C000178091

A Cynic's Guide to Management

A Cynic's Guide to Management

STUART McKIBBIN

ROBERT HALE · LONDON

ISBN 0 7090 6249 4

Robert Hale Limited
Clerkenwell House
Clerkenwell Green
London EC1R 0HT

2 4 6 8 10 9 7 5 3 1

Typeset in North Wales by
Derek Doyle & Associates, Mold, Flintshire.
Printed and bound by
WBC Book Manufacturers Limited, Bridgend

Contents

Introduction

Management education is one of the great growth occupations of our time. Books and auditoriums are regularly filled by so-called 'gurus' (many of whom have never actually managed so much as a mouse farm) propounding principles and techniques of successful management. It seems probable, however, that all these books and lectures have made more money for the authors than for their earnest disciples.

Heads stuffed with high-falutin' balderdash, clutching certificates that portentously proclaim them, on the strength of two years spent on some concrete campus in Neasden or Stoke Poges, 'Masters' of Business Administration, graduates of business schools return to the real world to wreak their own special kind of havoc in enterprises eager to employ them at the inflated salaries that their new-found (albeit so far entirely academic) mastery of business can command, thereby exemplifying one of the first laws of management: anticipated performance is paid better than achievement.

Many graduates of business schools find their way sooner or later (usually sooner) into the ranks of management consultants. Lack of any hardnosed practical experience, allied to an academic preference for theory over practice, along with an addiction to the heady pleasures of offering advice that is listened to respectfully (if only because of an uneasy awareness on the audience's part of the size of the bill that they will eventually receive for the advice), inclines them naturally towards this presumptuous profession.

What persuades any management to seek the views of total strangers on the way to run their business, based on investigation and research that is rarely intensive enough to provide a grasp of anything sharper than the wrong end of the stick, is a source of endless speculation. It intrigues particularly the unfortunate employees to whom will fall the thankless chore of attempting to put into practice the half-baked recommendations of the departing know-alls, entailing as it often does a heroic effort to reconcile the beautiful purity of the consultants' theories with the messy realities of the workplace and the limitations of the workforce.

Often it is disappointment with the organization's performance, a wistful belief that, given a new structure (consummated in the form of a new and resplendent organization chart), unsuspected reserves of ability and talent will be tapped, and doors opened wide on broad new vistas of profit and prestige.

The worm in this apparently succulent apple is of course that it ignores the capabilities and limitations of the people on the payroll. The beautifully constructed plan is based on the convenient but dangerous belief that people ought to conform to systems rather than the other way round.

As a result, what will usually happen is that the elegant system will soon be undermined by its unsuitability to the temperaments, abilities and talents of those who have to operate it. By then, of course, it will be too late to go back. The old bog-standard structure will have been comprehensively dismantled. Moreover, so much money will have been spent to implement the masterplan that considerations of 'face' alone will preclude any turning back. Stuck with an inappropriate structure, and working practices that are quite unsuited to the workers, the organization lurches on, wondering whatever happened to those new horizons so glowingly depicted in the chairman's annual report.

Rather like sex appeal, intelligence or some of the more obscure particles of molecular physics, good management is something that it is easier to define by its opposites and to recognize by its absence. And as might be expected, the pursuit of so elusive a goal has resulted in the evolution of many aberrant and idiosyncratic styles of management, each largely dependent on the culture that prevails within an organization, and on the attitudes and preferences of the people it employs.

In the following pages we take a look at some of them, and also at a few of the immutable laws of management and the disorders to which it is prone.

Styles of Management

FACED WITH EVIDENCE of failing corporate health, managers increasingly look for inspiration to the medical profession, and place their trust in what are essentially homeopathic remedies — treatment that produces symptoms like those of the disorder that it is hoped to cure.

Suppose, for example, that (as has happened in the NHS) proliferating ranks of bureaucrats are diverting resources from the main objective of the enterprise, the protection of health and the treatment of disease. Conventional therapy would involve such traditional measures as the wholesale dismissal of managers, clerks, accountants, 'efficiency experts' and human resources personnel in order to free space for patients and money for their treatment.

The homeopathic approach is quite different: involving such imaginative measures as reducing the number of clinical consultants and spending the money saved on management consultants. The diagnosis would in all probability be that the symptoms of ill-health are due, not to a surplus of bureaucrats but to a lack of controls on clinical expenditure.

From this diagnosis it can at once be seen what the homeopathic remedy would be: not fewer but more bureaucrats; the immediate creation of a further tier of managers to monitor and supervise the ways in which clinicians use their dwindling share of the fast-growing NHS budget.

As the fashion for this kind of treatment gains momentum it will surely not be long before Her

Homeopathic Management

FACED WITH EVIDENCE of failing corporate health, managers increasingly look for inspiration to the medical profession, and place their trust in what are essentially *homeopathic* remedies – treatment that produces symptoms like those of the disorder that it is hoped to cure.

Suppose, for example, that (as has happened in the NHS) proliferating ranks of bureaucrats are diverting resources from the main objective of the enterprise, the protection of health and the treatment of disease. Conventional therapy would involve such traditional measures as the wholesale dismissal of managers, clerks, accountants, 'efficiency experts' and human resources personnel in order to free space for patients, and money for their treatment.

The homeopathic approach is quite different, involving such imaginative measures as reducing the number of clinical consultants and spending the money saved on management consultants. The diagnosis would in all probability be that the symptoms of ill-health are due, not to a surplus of bureaucrats, but to a lack of controls on clinical expenditure.

From this diagnosis it can at once be seen what the homeopathic remedy would be: not fewer but *more* bureaucrats, the immediate creation of a further tier of managers to monitor and supervise the ways in which clinicians use their dwindling share of the fast-growing NHS budget.

As the fashion for this kind of treatment gains momentum it will surely not be long before Her

Majesty The Queen is graciously pleased to grant a charter establishing a Royal College of Homeopathic Management.

Ballcock Management

THE FAMILIAR DEVICE in a lavatory cistern provides the inspiration for a certain style of management. As everyone knows, when the pan is flushed the cistern is refilled by an inrush of water from the mains which ceases abruptly once the water reaches a predetermined level. The cut-off mechanism is of course the ballcock, borne upwards by the rising water level until, when the tank is full, it closes a valve to cut off the supply.

Some organizations resemble lavatory cisterns, being blessed (or cursed) with managers whose distinctive feature is that they operate like ballcocks. Although they themselves contribute little to the organization's success, they are for a long time kept afloat by the activities of others until the cut-off point is reached, at which they cease to rise. This happens when the supply of able subordinates dries up, as people tire of seeing their seniors take the credit for, and pocket the profits of, all their good ideas.

Narcissus Management

LIKE NARCISSUS GAZING spellbound at his own reflection in a pool, some managements are obsessed with their own image. What do customers and the general public think of them? Is the company as much admired as Marks and Spencer, or viewed with the same contempt as British Gas? How does it compare with Woolworths? These are questions to which managers yearn to have answers. To find them they employ market researchers to conduct an Image Survey.

Now some might think that the most reliable indication of corporate prestige, the esteem in which a company is held, would be its balance sheet. How people vote with their wallets shows pretty clearly what they think of a company's competitive position. This, however, is thought by managers to be a crude and unsophisticated way to measure the stature of a firm. Information that costs little or nothing is generally suspect. Only when a substantial fee has been paid to obtain it can information be regarded as reliable.

Hence the rapid growth of Narcissus Management, whose appetite for information concerning the corporate image extends now beyond the general public to embrace its own employees. 'What do they think of us?' wonders the Narcissus Manager as he surveys the respectful faces gathered round a meeting table, the blue-overalled ranks assembled in the works cafeteria, or the more subdued and genteel gathering in the staff canteen. Do they regard us as considerate employers? Do they think we are good at our jobs? Are they coming to work with a song in their hearts or a curse on their lips? Could it be (perish the thought!) that they think of us as prats?

The fact that employees are still on the payroll, that they haven't yet voted with their feet on management's performance, might be considered a reliable index of contentment. But what is needed to settle the management's mind is a substantial investment in a Staff Image Survey. Elaborate, detailed and confidential, this should reveal (at no small cost) conclusions that are deemed inaccessible to commonsense, among them the fact that few consider that they are generously (or even adequately) paid, that broad and clear careers paths stretch seductively before them, or that their energies and talents are properly rewarded with status and prestige. Staff, for their part, welcome an opportunity to beef and whinge about their employers in the company's time and at the management's expense.

A Staff Image Survey conducted for a company I worked for uncovered the fact that members of staff felt diffident about 'speaking up' to senior management. As somebody put it in one of those quotes so beloved of market researchers, 'speaking up can damage the health of your career!'

Deeply troubled by the findings of this survey, management lost no time in setting up a number of 'task forces', one of which was charged with finding ways of encouraging staff to speak their minds. After prolonged and anxious discussion the task forces duly pronounced themselves ready to report.

All, that is, except for the 'speaking up' task force. Although its members had indeed come up with any number of suggestions for ways of getting employees to speak up, not a single member of the task force was anxious to risk the disapproval of senior managers by putting his head above the parapet and acting as a spokesperson for the group.

The anxieties of Narcissus Management are rather like those of the adolescent afflicted with halitosis and acne, who worries incessantly about his popularity. But the great thing about an Image Survey, whether internal or external, is that, once carried out, it provides a bench-mark for comparison in subsequent years, enabling the sponsors to draw up an index of their popularity, anxiously watching its rises and falls across the years, and providing the market research firms who conduct these surveys with a reliable and steady source of income.

Evangelical Management

WHEN A COMPANY'S management feels impelled to declare its position, it often turns out in these days of managerial correctness to be the missionary position. Walk into the reception areas of many companies and your eye is likely to be caught by a notice in large type, proudly displayed in a prominent position. Under the heading 'Mission Statement' this proclaims in measured terms the company's dedication to such a range of social, ethical and moral values as might put a priest to shame.

As you read this high-flown masterpiece of Management Stately, you may or may not be impressed to learn of the organization's commitment to protecting the environment, to serving the local and national community, as well as to upholding every remotely relevant law and code of practice – in short, its dedication to being an all-round corporate good egg. Compared to a company's mission statement, a soldier's or judge's oath of allegiance to the monarch sounds almost non-committal. Not a hint of sordid commercial motivation is allowed to creep into a text that is more concerned to proclaim the company's selfless commitment to safeguarding the health and welfare of its staff, providing them with equal opportunities without favour being shown as to race, religion, gender, or mental and physical abilities.

It should be clear to visitors who read this document that they have entered a corporate heaven in which those fortunate enough to gain admission will spend blissful hours, enviably occupied in bringing good things to nice people.

Obsessed as so many of them are by current concepts

of managerial correctness, few companies feel that it is safe to operate without a filing cabinet stuffed with policies in support of their mission. The output of corporate policies can become prodigious. No aspect of human activity is considered too obscure or unimportant to be the subject of an official policy: on-site consumption of food and beverages, recreational use of computers, smoking (which, if permitted at all, will of course need to take place in approved locations designated for the purpose), holidays, training, company transport, alcoholic refreshment and many more.

Carefully and mellifluously worded (see **Management Rhetoric**) policies are the instruments through which a company declares the fulfilment of its mission. This avowed commitment to the socially and managerially correct doctrine of the day provides a respectable front behind which its employees can safely continue to indulge individual prejudices and preferences that may be far from correct – racist, homophobic, sexist and the rest. Policies provide the necessary camouflage for practice.

News Management

A FAMOUS, IF possibly apocryphal, exchange between
a foreign correspondent and his editor in London
dates back to the days before fax machines and other
technological advances replaced the cable as the medium
for transmitting urgent messages. Since cabled messages
were charged for by the word, it became common practice to run words together whenever possible. The
editor, a noted pedant who firmly believed that 'news'
was a plural noun, began the exchange by enquiring
politely, 'Are there any news?' Back came the prompt
reply: 'Not a single new!' 'Un-news, un-job' was the
editor's response. 'Up-shove job arsewards' replied the
journalist.

News is too scarce and valuable a commodity for an
adequate supply to be left entirely to chance. Every
newspaper you pick up, every TV and radio news
bulletin furnishes ample evidence of a serious shortage
of news. If enough headlines are to be contrived for the
radio and TV bulletins ('news on the hour every hour'),
if enough information is to be found to keep the margins
of newspapers apart, news needs to be purposefully
sought – and, if necessary, manufactured.

Deficiencies of drama in the news itself can often be
concealed by a dramatic presentation. In the case of
print, large headlines and a staccato style go far towards
convincing careless or superficial readers that events of
earth-shaking importance are being reported. If the news
is part of a report on TV or radio, the secret is to have it
presented not by a single news-reader or reporter, but by
a procession of them, each articulating carefully between
clenched teeth, a style of delivery now much in vogue

because it is thought to suggest both urgency and drama. The effect for which news editors strive is of a journalistic relay race in which the news baton passes swiftly from one hand to another: 'Simon Potter has the details' ... 'This report from Doris Morris' ... 'Here is Peter Patel' ... 'Over now to Croydon, where Jim Crow has the latest details' ... 'Jim Riddle has been watching events'. In this way one minuscule morsel of news can serve a whole journalistic food chain.

In times of particular scarcity, a reliable source of supply is 'the plant'. This works as follows: some obscure organization which has an axe to grind releases a report which journalists, desperate for a headline, seize on gratefully. Commonly, this tiny titbit purports to have been taken from a 'survey'. Such surveys occupy the time and energies of armies of surveyors, and no subject is too boring or obscure to be studied. Often what these surveys uncover is not what actually happens, but rather what, if it were to happen, would best justify their existence, be it ritual sacrifice of animals in Kent or child abuse in the West Riding of Yorkshire. Some surveys reveal what respondents think that other people think: '40% of parents believe that their children still believe in Father Christmas'.

The vocabulary of News Management is limited, leaning heavily, if not exclusively, on a number of words chosen from the *Guinness Book of Fatuous Hyperbole*: 'Agony of Gay Siamese Twin' ... 'Despair of Lonely Lighthouse Widow' ... 'Shame of Bonking Bishop'. (Emotions find their way into the headlines only in their most extreme and exaggerated form; thus, surprise is quickly promoted to Shock, pain to Agony, mild pleasure to Joy, and irritation to Fury.)

Territorial Management

LIKE MUCH OF creation, managers are driven by the territorial imperative, and defend their corporate territories with ferocious zeal.

Some animals delineate the margins of their patch with excrement, the hippopotamus, for instance, swishing its stumpy little tail rapidly from side to side to create a spray of ordure. Others, like foxes, splash their boundaries with urine. Birds warn off trespassers with song. Corporate animals have evolved more genteel adaptations of these techniques.

Companies threatened with being taken over by a predator throw out a barrage of literature which, while its purpose is defensive, is insultingly offensive to aggressive bidders, describing their offers in such pejorative terms as 'derisory' and 'totally inadequate'. Threatened by eviction from the comfortable nests that they have occupied for years, directors of the companies that others see as prey aim streams of shrill invective at their enemies, while deluging allies with fancifully optimistic profit forecasts. Companies which have performed disappointingly for years suddenly issue promises of balance sheets transformed by 'a new focus' and 'dynamic leadership'. Shareholders who remain loyal are offered bribes no less tempting for being funded with their own money.

Within an organization, savage internecine battles for territory are waged with memoranda, reports, position papers and incessant lobbying activities. Creative accountancy enables figures to be massaged in ways that serve the purposes of ambitious managers. Not for nothing has the process of continuous, subtle denigration of colleagues by managers competing to expand their empires at the expense of rivals come to be known as dropping each other 'in the shit'.

The progress of internal territorial struggles, both for staff and for whole departments, can be followed by studying the organization charts, which faithfully reflect the outcome of these power struggles. Boxes linked by solid and dotted lines in a complicated pattern reveal with merciless clarity the current pecking order, showing who reports to whom. As in every other corner of the jungle, only the fittest survive, the fittest being managers who achieve the ultimate territorial ambition of taking over somebody else's department, company or group.

Inflation Management

INFLATION MANAGEMENT CAN best be described as the art of making a six-course banquet out of a cheese sandwich. Its results can be observed in many walks of life, even in those as mundane as television weather forecasts. At one time, these used to consist of displaying a readily intelligible outline map of the British Isles, divided into segments. Each of these contained a terse verbal forecast for that area: 'sunny spells and showers', 'persistent rain', etc.

These days, such easy-to-understand forecasts have been replaced by a form of meteorological showbiz presentation, a Weather Forecast Show, choreographed for visual enjoyment with simpering bimbos and sharply suited male 'presenters' performing a kind of weather ballet in front of largely incomprehensible satellite pictures. Pictured against a constantly changing backdrop of weather maps, these people grin and wink at us like stand-up comedians. What used to occupy thirty seconds now takes about five minutes. The weather forecast has been inflated into a programme in its own right.

In education the inflationary process takes two forms. One is the creeping pretentiousness of the process by which humble institutions are verbally exalted. What used to be called a 'technical college' acquires the title (but not the status) of 'university'. The second form of educational inflation is debasement of the currency. Just as you now have to fork out a fiver for what, a few years ago, would have cost you five shillings, the diplomas, certificates, and degrees of schools and universities today have lost a great deal of their value. Someone who leaves university now with a second-class degree is probably no better educated than one who left school twenty years ago with a good school certificate.

It is not all that long since students leaving school could embark at once on training for a profession such as medicine, accountancy or law. Now these professions are barred to anyone unable to produce a university degree. This does not, as is often claimed, mean that standards of entry are now higher; what it shows is a desperate attempt to protect these professions from the ravages of educational inflation.

Hostage Management

IF YOU CAN be called directly to account for profits and results, you are in a highly vulnerable position. What you need to do, without delay, is find someone to interpose between the coal-face and yourself. True, your current situation does enable you to claim all the credit for success. But against this advantage you have to set the considerable risk that you alone can be held responsible for failure.

Hence the need to find a hostage, a human shock-absorber on whose shoulders you will be able to load the blame for any failure. With a bit of luck, you should still be able to lay claim to a substantial share of the credit for success.

Taking a hostage, someone willing to sacrifice his career for yours, to see his reputation perish in order that yours may survive, calls for substantial diplomatic skills. The most promising approach is flattery. A proposal along these lines will often procure you a hostage: 'Guy, I've been hugely impressed by the results that you've achieved and by the progress you've made. I can tell you it's no secret that others share my admiration, so I had no trouble in persuading the board that the time has come to recognize your ability. I am therefore putting you in operational control of sales, allowing me to concentrate on strategic direction.'

By craftily coupling your role with the adjective 'strategic' you should still be able to attribute to your own vision and far-sighted planning a large measure of any successes. At the same time disasters or serious embarrassments can be put down to 'operational failures' by your designated hostage.

Defensive Management

EVERY DECISION HAS a down-side in the form of substantial potential for failure, or even disaster. So faced with a need to take any decision, the Defensive Manager will rapidly seek to implicate others in the process.

The classic device for sharing responsibility for a decision is, of course, to set up a committee. Let's say that you have been asked to make a key appointment; the consequences of hiring someone who turns out to be a dud could be hugely damaging and embarrassing.

What then should you do? The answer is to set up a 'selection committee'. Colleagues will more easily be persuaded to join you on the committee if you explain that you respect and value their judgement of people. It will probably help to implicate one or two people who qualify as 'experts' – a psychologist perhaps, or a 'leadership consultant'. If desperate, you can even call in a handwriting expert.

Once you have assembled your panel of (in the legal sense) 'accessories' you'll have ensured that, if your collective choice proves unsuccessful, no one will ever be able to pin the blame on you. If on the other hand the appointee proves successful you can always explain to the board that, as chairman of the selection committee, your own preference was decisive in persuading your fellow members to make the right choice.

Cuckoo Management

B E WARY OF accepting help from other managers, and be careful who you hire as an assistant. A bad decision could make you a victim of Cuckoo Management. Just as most murders are committed by members of the victim's family or by someone known to him, most fatal attacks on a manager's career are committed by close colleagues.

The classic scenario for Cuckoo Management goes like this: a manager whose department seems to be in trouble is urged to accept an assistant, 'someone who can take on the job of meeting short-term targets, leaving you free to take the longer view essential to the continuing health of this great company of ours'. A proposition in such terms from a senior member of the board is often hard to resist.

Unfortunately most companies are run by fast buck merchants. It is what happens today, this year, that counts. Let the future look after itself. However sound your long-term planning, however far-seeing you may be, if your new assistant is successful in meeting or over-shooting short-term targets, he or she will rapidly over-take you in status and rewards. Before too long you may find yourself evicted from your departmental nest, while the cuckoo stays on to hatch out all your carefully laid long-term eggs.

Another dangerous proposal runs along these lines: 'Look, George, you're such a talented, creative guy that you shouldn't have to carry any of the burdens of administration. On the other hand (though of course he is not in the same creative league as you) Cecil has a proven ability to handle all the administrative chores that you must find so irksome. Why don't we form an alliance of his department and your own, making you responsible only for the creative bit?'

Sounds reasonable, attractive even, but if you are unwise enough to accept the proposal (you may have no choice but to do so, but that's another issue) you will rapidly discover that the humble duties of administration include such crucial functions as hiring and firing staff, fixing their remuneration and deciding on promotions. All that you'll be left with is the thankless task of getting first-class work out of second-rate people. Before long, the cuckoo's department will have been merged with your own, and guess who will be in sole occupation of the nest, using the now much-expanded departmental budget to stuff his favourites with corporate titbits like company cars, and promoting the interests of his loyal fledglings.

The corridors of advertising agencies are full of the casualties of Cuckoo Management.

Crisis Management

CRISIS MANAGEMENT CONSISTS not in resolving crises, but in manufacturing them. Like others of my generation, I was raised in the comfortable belief that we British are at our best in a crisis. Implicit in this belief was the curious conviction that we, uniquely, possess the qualities of energy, resourcefulness, courage, initiative, imagination and the ability to improvise, to be able to rise triumphantly to the kind of challenges that ordinary, humdrum, everyday life fails to provide.

Possibly some vestigial remnant of this charming piece of folklore accounts for the alacrity with which some managers elevate to the status of a crisis some minor mishap or trivial misfortune. Perhaps they hanker nostalgically for the opportunity to give of their best which only a full-blooded, 22-carat crisis can provide. Unfortunately it is this aspect of our traditional response to a crisis, a masterful ability to cope, that we seem now to have lost. All that remains is an extraordinary talent for escalating misfortunes into crises. It takes little more than a flurry of snow to bring the country to a standstill. Trains run late, if at all, roads become impassable, and dire warnings are issued by the authorities to stay at home unless your journey is 'essential'.

Our rich vocabulary is plundered for hyperbole, words sufficiently redolent of urgency and drama to convey the true dimensions of the awful crisis that we face. Spokespersons vie with each other in exaggeration. The kind of winter conditions that would pass unnoticed in North America are described by the AA as 'diabolical'. 'It's a white hell out there' responds the

RAC, not to be outdone. While a spokesman for the railways weighs in with the grave (and probably accurate) assertion that the disruption to services is 'the worst on record'.

On the available evidence, it is beginning to look as if our national talent for rising to a crisis has become little more than a singular capacity for creating one.

Meddle Management

LIKE CARS, MOST organizations are inherently stable. Without too much movement of the steering wheel or sudden applications of the brakes or throttle, they will continue to pursue a relatively steady, even course.

When this is diverted or interrupted by what has come to be known euphemistically as 'hands on' management, the results can be disastrous. What the hands are on is of course the steering wheel as the driver wrenches it convulsively from side to side, alternately hitting the brakes and stepping on the gas.

In Meddle Management we see management in its purest form, compulsively and perpetually altering, fidgeting and tampering, a monstrous regiment of tinkerers, meddlers and fiddlers whose ill-timed and misguided interference is ruining many a business.

Meddle managers derive their inspiration from a book by 'Management Guru' Sir John Harvey-Jones entitled *Making It Happen*. Fired by the author's distinguished record of management success with an unhealthy enthusiasm for intervention, the Meddle Manager devotes his life to causing happenings that should never occur, never pausing for a moment to reflect that the company would be far better off if they didn't happen at all.

The most immediately evident characteristic of Meddle Management is its love of relocation, moving people and offices around. While changes in management structure (reallocation of responsibilities) are a common form of interference, they lack the advantage of being immediately visible to all. At first they are made manifest only in the organization chart, a document close to the heart of every Meddle Manager who delights in constantly redrawing the lines that show who reports to whom, and in adding little boxes to the chart. On the other hand, moving people about between offices and buildings is an infinitely more satisfying form of interference because its consequences are instantly and universally apparent.

Moving people about has one other major attraction: most movements are reversible. People can be moved back to offices from which they were evicted; ceilings but recently lowered can be raised again; and partitions erected at no small cost can be no less expensively demolished. The incessant noise, piles of rubble and dust-filmed surfaces create an impression of dynamism. Perpetual motion has been established, with people on the move creating an illusion of a company that is going places.

Alibi Management

LIKE A BONE-WEARY traveller sinking thankfully into a favourite armchair, Alibi Management collapses gratefully into the warm and comforting embrace of an excuse.

This is a style of management most often met in the public utilities and services. The most accomplished practitioners are employed by the railways, the management of which has become astonishingly adept at parading before their incredulous, long-suffering customers a litany of alibis which range across the whole spectrum of failure – human, mechanical and electrical. These excuses are communicated over the public address systems of stations and, occasionally, trains.

However, due to management's reluctance to give those who offer such excuses to the public even the most elementary training in composition, diction and pronunciation, they are usually difficult and sometimes impossible to understand. Impenetrable though most of these announcements are (since they contrive to be at the same time illiterate, inarticulate and incoherent), regular travellers soon become skilled at interpreting the excuses they are offered: 'staff shortages' (some lazy bugger has failed to turn up for work), 'an incident at Penge' (their incompetence has driven some poor sod to suicide), 'signalling problems' (combination of inadequate maintenance and incompetent employees), 'traction difficulties' (our old friend, leaves on the line), 'severe weather conditions' (the wrong kind of snow), and, finally, that jackpot of excuses, 'reaction to the failure of a previous train, and non-arrival of the carriages to form your train'.

Railway customers are seldom spoken to directly, except occasionally by a guard eager to emulate the style of address made familiar by cabin crew on aircraft: 'We are now commencing the approach to Euston' . . . 'This is your steward speaking'. When, as happens all too often, your train is inexplicably marooned in some rural wilderness, the closest you are ever likely to get to an explanation is an impenetrable twittering on the intercom as guard and driver commune anxiously together. 'This train will now be fast to London' is an often repeated assertion that flatly contradicts the almost universal experience that the only fast things on the entire railway system are the station clocks.

An interesting mutation of Alibi Management is Capitulation Management, an advanced form in which management becomes so resigned to failure that it turns away from all the problems of business, devoting its attention to devising ways of increasing management remuneration without attracting too much unsympathetic attention.

Signal Management

SIGNAL MANAGERS BELIEVE that every action sends a message. Like the disintegrating family which puts on, for Christmas, funerals and weddings, a brave show of unity and harmony, Signal Management is more concerned with appearances than reality. Its greatest fear is of 'sending the wrong kind of signals'. However, since unspoken messages are even more susceptible to misinterpretation than those articulated in either speech or print, the Signal Manager is constantly beset by doubts concerning the nature of the messages conveyed by his actions and decisions. Stepping gingerly through the mine-field of possible misinterpretations, Signal Managers have to consider, not just the consequences that flow directly from decisions that they take, but, of more pressing concern, the nature of the signals that they thereby send to friend and foe.

A classic case of Signal Management that I observed centred on an apparently innocent and innocuous decision with (one would have thought) little potential for controversy. A large international company decided to hold a conference, to be attended by participants from a number of countries. Where to hold the meeting, a simple enough decision most people might imagine, being simply a matter of striking a reasonable balance between cost, convenience, facilities and comfort, was entrusted to a senior manager of the Signal tendency who lost no time in identifying the hidden risk of 'sending the wrong kind of signals'.

Of the various venues suggested for the meeting, easily the most attractive was a hotel situated in a French resort. This offered not only the most desirable and convenient location, the best facilities for a large meeting and the highest standard of cuisine, but also (because the meeting was to be held during winter months) the lowest cost in the shape of special out-of-season rates. This almost ideal venue was however turned down by Signal Management in favour of a more expensive establishment in Paris.

This perverse decision was explained on the grounds that the less expensive hotel was situated in a world-famous resort (yet another good reason, some might imagine, to hold the meeting there). However, terrified by the thought of sending staff and shareholders throughout the world the message that a few employees were living high off the hog at a famous French resort, the management opted for a costlier, less attractive alternative in Paris – a decision that it justified on the grounds that the firm had an office in the capital. The substantial extra bill was considered a small premium to pay for insurance against the risk of 'sending the wrong kind of signal'.

Abdication Management

WHAT (YOU MIGHT ask) could be more engagingly humble than to transfer to a total stranger the responsibility for managing your business? Inviting an outsider to come in and run it sounds almost Oriental in the self-effacing humility that it suggests. It is reminiscent of the Japanese Prime Minister who, not long ago, resigned on the quite unprecedented grounds that he didn't feel up to the job. (Imagine any British manager or politician quitting office, admitting to the total failure of his tenure, even when, as is usually the case, this is plain for all to see.)

Some senior managers, however, are less arrogant. They know that experience of the business and an intimate knowledge of the people it employs, do not equip them to run it. It is this rare quality of humility which, combined with a wistful belief in magic, persuades so many organizations to bring in management consultants.

Specialists in the art of minding other people's business, consultants thrive on the reluctance of Abdication Managers to make their own decisions, even when it is patently obvious what these ought to be. So when, in due course, the decisions are recommended, the blame can be laid squarely on the shoulders of the consultants, along with any odium to which the consequences may give rise.

Even when the obvious action is not unpopular, the consultants still serve a useful function: the size of their fee provides the necessary reassurance that the decisions to be taken are indeed the right ones. Had they been taken without incurring this substantial extra cost, the management would always have been subject to self-doubt.

Abdication Management believes that the best decisions are those that cost the most.

Obstruction Management

THE JOYS OF Obstruction Management appeal particularly to the kind of busybodies who are attracted to work in government, national or local. The impulse to meddle compulsively in other people's lives is more readily indulged when some ostensible social benefit can be used to camouflage it.

An example is road safety. Because this is something which everybody favours, it can be cited as the reason for all kinds of interference with the smooth flow of traffic. Citation of this wholly commendable aim can be used to fend off criticism by diverting attention from the actual merits of the means chosen to achieve it. The mere mention of road safety should be enough to explain and justify the gross inconvenience to which road users are constantly subjected. Placards announcing 'traffic calming' measures proliferate alarmingly in quiet, narrow suburban streets where speeding is anyway made impossible by rows of cars parked on either side. Minuscule white pimples known as 'mini roundabouts' are painted at crossroads to interrupt the flow of traffic.

For the kind of people who find making difficulties enjoyable and satisfying, Obstruction Management offers countless opportunities.

Convoy Management

DESPITE ALL THE brave talk about 'managing change' and 'the accelerating pace of change', the unfashionable fact remains that, like wartime convoys, most organizations proceed at the pace of their slowest constituent, the slowest in this instance being the slowest-witted managers. Amid all the fashionable techno-babble and trendy electronics (video conferences, surfing the Internet, working from a home- or car-based office, etc.) there are still mail order companies incapable of taking orders on the telephone, or of bringing together on a single bill a number of separate purchases made by a credit customer. The strongest gravitational pull in most organizations is exerted by *precedent*. 'This is the way we have always done it' is still thought to be an assertion to settle any argument.

Conversely, the most powerful corporate motivation is not ambition, sex or greed; it is fear of innovation. Corporate man has evolved a whole range of well-proven devices for resisting innovation, procrastinating and slowing down the pace of change. Just as governments set up enquiries as an excuse for doing nothing, organizations have committees, working parties, study groups and the incongruously named task force. Between them, these are calculated to postpone to the millennium and beyond any decisive step forward in a new direction.

Managers feel safer in a convoy, particularly if its progress is imperceptible.

Beehive Management

MODELLED, AS THE name suggests, on the social structures of the insect world, Beehive Managers fall into one or other of three categories: workers, drones and queens, of which the second is by far the biggest. Large corporations such as British Gas and the various privatized utilities are particularly likely to practise this style of management.

At the heart of the hive's complex social organization is the corpulent figure of the chief executive or queen, whose protection and nourishment is the duty and privilege of the other insects. Interestingly, in the corporate mutation of hive society there may be more than one queen, a role sometimes assumed not only by the chairman, but also by other members of the board.

At times when adequate nourishment is in short supply, the queens are obliged to compete for sustenance, the location and transport of which is the function of the workers. When a fresh source of supply is located, the finders return to the hive whose other occupants assemble to witness and participate in an elaborate 'dance' involving endless meetings attended by the drones who engage in an intricate process of assembling and dividing into groups and subgroups. The function of these is to conduct a continuous debate concerning the size and quality of the new source, and the likelihood of its resources proving large enough to satisfy the gargantuan appetites of the ever-swelling queens.

Another challenge that greatly exercises these small groups is that of reconciling the ingenuity of the remuneration committee and accountants with the scruples of the non-executive directors.

Virtual Management

WE HEAR A lot about what is called 'virtual reality' – an experience so vividly simulated with the aid of a computer that, were it not for our knowledge that the things we see and the sounds we hear are being artificially produced, we could almost believe that we are in fact flying an aircraft or touring the corridors of a building for real.

This simulation of reality is a popular technique of management: meetings are set up, discussions are held, responsibilities defined, people relocated, functions reassigned and organization charts redrawn. 'Job evaluation' schemes are introduced, and much time occupied with 'performance appraisals'. In addition, staff not engaged in any of these forms of Work Replacement Therapy (q.v.) occupy their time with training programmes.

Of these there'll be many to choose from (see **The Law of Peripheral Primacy**). And if none of these appeal there will also be 'efficiency audits', and 'management development workshops'.

All the motions, in fact, are gone through in a way that is uncannily convincing until the realization dawns that all this frenetic activity is an elaborate charade in which the word that is being mimed is 'management'. People co-operate in the pretence for mutual support; their self-esteem, in fact, depends on the illusion of dynamic, purposeful activity. What gives the game away, and alerts you to the fact that apparent reality is only virtual, is the gap between plan and execution, objective and method. At the end of the day, none of the activity observed results in better products, more effective selling methods or larger profits.

Displacement Management

MANAGERS OFTEN FIND too daunting the problems involved in running an efficient, profitable business. This is why, in a number of organizations, energies once harnessed to such traditional functions as manufacturing a product or delivering a service at a profit become diverted to more modish and enjoyable activities that make fewer demands on energy or intellect.

Of these, one of the most popular is training. This is perhaps best defined as the function of equipping people to perform superbly tasks that they will probably never have to carry out in conditions that they will never actually face. Indeed, the more irrelevant to their everyday functions the activities that trainees are asked to undertake, the greater the value that is placed on the training process, and the larger the investment in it.

A simple example may help to illustrate the point. Take the case of 'creatives' in the advertising business. To train them in the challenging but mundane task of creating halfway decent ads that manage to sell their clients' products without patronizing consumers or insulting their intelligence might seem an appropriate objective for a course of training. Displacement Management would, however, find this too much of a challenge. Instead, designers and copywriters are forced, protesting, into wet suits, preparatory to going snorkelling on Lake Windermere. Startled accountants find themselves dangling at the end of ropes as they make panic-stricken efforts to abseil down a cliff, while a terrified marketing manager fights off claustrophobia as he crawls painfully along a muddy concrete drainpipe.

Of course, not all training exercises need be so physically demanding. Provided that they satisfy the basic requirement of irrelevance, they can be purely sedentary. Bookkeepers are winkled from their solitary cubicles to be forcibly trained in 'Communication Skills'. 'Assertiveness Training' is arranged for the receptionists, and courses in 'Leadership', provided for commissionaires (who at least have the advantage of a resplendent uniform). The maintenance manager is driven from his office to attend a course in 'Public Speaking'.

Nobody with experience of corporate life will need to be reminded that only a small proportion of the working week can ever be devoted to useful or profitable activities. In most organizations, time is far more enjoyably occupied in a whole range of the Displacement activities that have now become so fashionable.

Job Evaluation

The uninitiated might assume that, for example, greeting visitors and recording their time of arrival and departure is not a particularly difficult task to accomplish with reasonable speed and success. Displacement Managers know better. Rather than rely on commonsense, the Displacement Manager will not rest content until the operation has been minutely analysed in such elaborate detail that the receptionist's job assumes on paper the apparent dimensions of the chief executive's.

Performance Reviews

As we shall see later, actual work occupies only a portion of the working year. How large this is will be determined by the growing proportion of each employee's time that is devoted to discussing how they do it. These intimate discussions are by no means one-sided. Not only do managers take the trouble to tell staff in great detail how they think they are doing their jobs; in the more progressive organizations, staff are now encouraged to tell superiors how they seem to be doing *their* jobs. In consequence, members of staff spend a great deal of their time reviewing each other's performance and recording their remarks on voluminous forms. Whether or not these are ever read by anyone is open to serious doubt. Nor does it greatly matter. The point is that reviews of performance, whether upward or downward, occupy a lot of time.

Working Parties

The word 'committee' is now hopelessly outdated; bureaucratic ingenuity has come up with scores of dynamic-sounding euphemisms such as 'working party' and 'study group'. Invitations to join these gatherings are greatly prized, and again provide endless opportunities for occupying time in a congenial and harmless way that involves no great expenditure of energy or skill. (Much of corporate life is of a social rather than commercial nature.)

When establishments like stores and banks close their doors to customers during normal working hours, explaining that the closure is for purposes of 'staff training', Displacement Management has clearly won the upper hand. How long, one wonders, will it be before schools close to pupils in order to carry out 'staff education'?

Lifeboat Management

THE NATURE OF Lifeboat Management is best explained by a fable.

Following the wreck of their ship in a typhoon, surviving members of the crew set sail in a lifeboat. Lacking charts and maps (all lost in the storm) the captain asks some of the survivors to form a 'navigation task force', charged with setting a course for the nearest land. Others are made members of a 'victuals study group' whose function is to look after what stocks of food and water were salvaged from the wreck.

The remaining survivors form an 'oarsmen's working party'. To them falls the key responsibility of keeping the boat on the move. After protracted debate, the navigation task force comes up with a recommended course. However, the boat, being heavily loaded, the victuals study group complain that the meagre supplies on board will be insufficient for the voyage. Meanwhile the oarsmen assert that the energies they expend to keep the vessel on the move entitle them to extra rations.

At this point, management (in the person of the skipper) intervenes. He decrees that the boat is too heavily loaded, and that, with the greatest regret, he is going to be compelled to down-size its crew and let some of the complement go. He explains, however, that he wishes to be fair to all, and to ensure that the burden of redundancy is shared equally between navigators, victuallers and oarsmen. Accordingly, one member of each group would be asked to join an 'equal sacrifice committee' whose job is to choose individuals destined for early release.

49

Next the victuallers come up with an idea. With fewer mouths to feed, they suggest, the requirement for food and water will be proportionately lessened. Why not, therefore, lighten the load still further by jettisoning surplus supplies? The skipper votes this a great idea, and soon, following the departure of selected members of the crew, the surface of the sea is littered with casks of water and kegs of food.

Not wishing to be outdone by their shipmates, the oarsmen too have a proposal. Since there were now fewer of them, would it not make sense to get rid of surplus oars? These, too, are now discarded including one at the stern which, as someone points out, is not performing its natural function since it is only being used by the navigator as a tiller.

Within a short space of time, the boat, with its now much-depleted crew, is being rowed contentedly round and round in circles, with those on board engaged in continuous debate concerning their plans for the future as soon as a landfall is achieved.

Lacking replenishment, victuals and energies drain relentlessly away, thus bringing to an end the first recorded instance of a now common management style.

Placebo Management

THE DICTIONARY DEFINES a placebo as: 'Anything lacking intrinsic remedial value done or given to humour another'.

This definition calls instantly to mind a number of management practices and institutions. A popular placebo is the 'boardroom lunch', attended as it is not by all, or even most, members of the board, but by one or two of their number who have been deputed to entertain, to rollmops followed by jubilee chicken, a representative selection of 'ordinary' employees. Wearing their best suits and nervous smiles, guests are invited to speak their minds, with tongues loosened by a glass or two of vinegary Muscadet, on topics related to their work. Intimidated as most of them naturally are by the setting and the hosts' seniority they are unlikely to be too critical or candid. But the illusion that their views could influence events or policy that the occasion creates is considered by management to be therapeutic in the typical way of a placebo. (It is therapeutic, also, for the senior managers present, who, in the habitual absence of serious criticism from their guests, feel entitled to assume that all is going swimmingly.)

The staff committee is another institution whose main placebo effect lies in the opportunity that it provides to hold elections. Each department is invited to elect one or two representatives to the committee, which meets regularly to discuss such uncontroversial topics as the provision of flu inoculations and the progress of the darts team. By giving all members of the staff opportunities to vote, the company contrives to generate a therapeutic illusion of democracy, rather as if voters at a national referendum on the EEC were invited to express a preference for the colour of its flag.

Although the use of placebos is no longer considered respectable in medical circles, they continue to play a central role in current management practice.

Puppet Management

LIKE CHARLIE MCCARTHY and Archie Andrews, ventriloquists' dummies often achieve much greater fame than the talented people who manipulate them and supply them with a voice. In the same way, corporate puppet masters have to learn to remain content with influencing people and events at one remove. Though they will never get the credit, puppet masters have the satisfaction of knowing that it is they who call the shots, writing the speeches and proposals, coming up with ideas for which their dummies have to be allowed to take the credit.

Lending a fluent voice or pen to senior members of staff makes it possible for the inarticulate to speak and enables the illiterate to write persuasively – a satisfying and rewarding form of charitable work. The only drawback from the managerial puppet's point of view is the ever-present danger that the ventriloquist may come up with plans or policies that prove highly controversial, thus committing the puppet to some course of action that he does not really wish to take. However handicapped by lack of intelligence or education, the ambitious manager is well advised to acquire some skill with words.

Zoological Management

STUDENTS OF MANAGEMENT soon spot an intriguing resemblance between the worlds of management and nature. Here are just a few:

Hamster Management

Mention of the hamster brings instantly to mind a vision of a little creature obsessively spinning the wheel in its cage. And anyone who has ever watched a hamster on its treadmill cannot fail to have noticed the resemblance to a familiar management style. The creature's obsessive but fruitless attempts to ascend the wheel rotating in its cage are a powerful reminder of the strenuous but purposeless activity that provides some managers with the comforting illusion of achievement. The effort involved in keeping the treadmill turning absorbs their energies in a satisfying way which effectively obscures the fact that they are getting nowhere. Busyness rather than business is the goal at which they aim with an endless, self-perpetuating cycle of meetings and video conferences, working parties, study groups, feasibility studies, steering groups and all the rest, to say nothing of the prodigious efforts that they are obliged to make in an endless struggle to surmount the piles of paperwork that they generate. Symbiotic relationships are formed which keep some occupied full-time in producing the mountain of paperwork that others feel obliged to read.

Industrious, obstinate and hugely energetic, but lacking the capacity to learn from experience, the hamster spends a lifetime pedalling happily away.

Seagull Management

A style of management well known to those who work for a subsidiary of a foreign parent company. A bird of passage flies over from head office, spending no longer with the locals than is needed to crap all over them before departing to do the same at another destination.

Locust Management

Locust Management is the favoured style of companies that specialize in taking over others. When successful, they can strip the companies for which they bid of every single asset, leaving empty husks and a network of branches picked clean of every tasty morsel.

Peacock Management

Who could be so mean of spirit as to withhold admiration from the Peacock Manager as he struts proudly before his audience of shareholders and staff? Who would suspect of a creature that looks so sleek and complacent the ability to take off so suddenly and fly to a loftier perch? The droppings that it leaves behind in such profusion testify to the rich and ample diet provided by its former keepers.

Rabbit Management

Named after the legendary reproductive powers of the species, Rabbit Management is widely practised by large international firms.

The typical pattern of Rabbit Management is roughly as follows. All the functions represented on the organization chart of the parent company are then reproduced locally in each of its subsidiaries abroad. Thus, if the parent company has sales and marketing directors, so too will the companies in Japan, Australia, Germany, France, Italy and the UK.

However, unless the management is impotent or sterile, it will continue to reproduce. First, a separate 'global' management structure is set up in parallel to the structure of the parent and subsidiaries to supervise their activities. Later, as these subsidiaries proliferate, they are assembled in regional groups with a regional management structure which, again, replicates the local, global and parental structures.

This means that if all the offspring survive (and they nearly always do) there will be a sales and marketing director at parental, national, regional and global levels to get in each other's way and interfere in each other's decisions, each with his own premises and subordinate employees.

As this example shows, the fabled reproductive capacities of the rabbit can easily be matched by ambitious managers.

Prosthetic Management

THE SUPPLY OF artificial parts to remedy deficiencies is one of the crucial functions of enlightened management. This is why that common deficiency, intelligence, has now so many prosthetic replacements in the shape of electronic gadgets.

These range in complexity from the bar code readers and pocket calculators that compensate for the inability of check-out staff (the hapless products of progressive education) either to read or add up prices on the cartons that they process, to the more sophisticated forms of ersatz intelligence on which senior managers can call.

Some have revolutionized the role of management to such an extent that chaos, once the random product of management decisions, is now, in the shape of Chaos Theory, an influential component of scientific management.

For writers and designers, whose individual creations so often betray a conspicuous deficiency of talent, word-processors and Apple Macs offer prosthetic replacements for what might otherwise have proved a distressing inability to spell or draw.

Already, word-processors are available that can reproduce in print a message spoken to them. This development in prosthetic science holds out the promise of completing the process, already so far advanced by many of our schools, of removing forever the stigma of illiteracy, enabling the illiterate to compete on equal terms with those who have learned so painfully to write. All that now remains is for science to devise a prosthetic replacement for the ability to read, a machine that is able to scan and speak a printed text, eliminating at a stroke the unfair disadvantages currently suffered by those who cannot read.

Disorders of Management

Feline Obesity Syndrome

SO-CALLED BECAUSE of the resemblance to fat cats that sufferers are said to acquire, this is a disease of our times. Its onset is characterized by sudden, often spectacular, gains in weight that are out of all proportion to the stature of the victim. A characteristic early symptom is a pronounced distortion of the victim's stance and gait, caused by an unsightly, fast-growing distension of the wallet, of which the rapid increase in weight and size soon tends to give the sufferer a distinctly lop-sided appearance. Insatiable hunger is another early symptom: patients' appetite for financial reward is often mistaken for greed, with the result that they suffer the humiliation and indignity not just of being mocked as 'fat cats', but also of insensitive and hurtful references to snouts and trotters in the trough. The regrettable result is that victims of this unfortunate and increasingly common condition are denied the same degree of public sympathy that other maladies command.

The typical victim is a relatively minor functionary in a corporation, often a public utility that has recently been privatized. The sudden additional strain and responsibility of doing exactly the same job for a private, rather than a public, monopoly is thought to render managers of modest and sometimes even imperceptible abilities peculiarly vulnerable to approaches from predatory bidders, so anxious to secure their services that they would be prepared to offer prodigious rewards. In consequence, an appetite that was once more than satisfied by a modest rise in salary soon rapidly expands to encompass enormous bonuses, generous share options, huge pension contributions and indeed the whole broad spectrum of corporate rewards.

To pre-empt such approaches from outside, and in order to maintain what is customarily described as the company's competitive position, the manager (hitherto someone regarded as no more than a minor bureaucrat in an obscure utility) is suddenly forced to accept extravagant rewards on which the full glare of national publicity is soon bound to fall.

Managers thus suddenly enriched often have to make sacrifices in the line of duty, moving, for example, to homes in the top Council Tax brackets, or having to pay the heavier expenses of running larger cars. Others find themselves having to face the ever-present risk of suffering a fatal injury as a result of diving into an empty swimming pool.

Reluctant though sufferers may be to accept the burdens and responsibilities of wealth, they tend to be individuals of outstanding public spirit, who shoulder such duties unselfishly in the interests of others, to provide (as they like to explain) a target for their juniors to aim at, and to enable managers of lower rank and even more modest capabilities to be more generously paid.

It is important to recognize the wholly altruistic motivation of sufferers from Feline Obesity Syndrome, the depredations of which malady are by no means confined to the private corporate sector. Many other fields of public life afford examples of substantially increased rewards being reluctantly accepted in the interests of others – consumers, tax-payers, voters or simply the public at large. MPs, for instance, vote themselves substantial salary increases only in order to maintain the quality of the people who choose to serve the nation in this way. Without substantially increased remuneration, the electorate would not be able to count on being represented by members of the intellectual and moral stature so conspicuous in members of the current parliament.

It is a tragic revelation of public cynicism that men and women prepared to shoulder the burdens of sudden, unearned wealth should be derided when they display the symptoms of what is, after all, simply an occupational disease.

Furor Pecuniae (Wage-rage)

ALTHOUGH THE CAUSES and symptoms are similar, there are two distinct forms of this disease to which organizations such as trade unions are particularly prone. Both are caused by an identical conviction that a wage or salary has been incorrectly fixed, that it is inappropriate to the skill and contribution of the worker. If the wage in question is that of the victim, the disease is known as *Outrage*, in which form it can lead to marches, demonstrations and other forms of noisy public protest, accompanied by figure-massage on an epic scale to ensure that the victim's current wage (which may well in fact be substantially enlarged by a complex package of bonuses, overtime payments and allowances) is cosmetically reduced in size in order to make it seem derisory.

Thus, the by no means insubstantial wages of a teacher (whose seasonally adjusted teaching year works out at about eight months, and who enjoys more paid holiday than employees in any other occupation in the country) are energetically massaged by the union spokesman until, by comparison, a Bombay rickshaw coolie seems well paid. Nurses too (whose skills often approximate less closely to those of a brain surgeon than to those required of an office cleaner, or factory first-aid worker) parade in vociferous protest at the size of a salary increase that many of the self-employed would envy.

The second form of Wage-rage, *Umbrage* is generated when the emoluments of others are considered too substantial. The difference between the salary of the sufferer and that paid to the individual with whom he chooses to compare it (typically, the chairman of a privatized utility) is described in strident terms as 'bloated' or 'obscene' (see **Feline Obesity Syndrome**).

Although the symptoms of this form of Furor are often hard to distinguish from the simple, non-pathological emotion Envy, it is in fact a morbid condition that can cause considerable distress.

Olsen's Disease

NAMED AFTER A former chief executive of Cunard who achieved international fame for masterminding the famous 'floating building site' voyage of the *QE2* for which hundreds of passengers paid premium rates in order to cross the Atlantic in conditions scarcely less uncomfortable than those endured by travellers who made the same voyage on board the *Mayflower*. This epic voyage cost Cunard about £8 million in compensation payments and their chief executive his job. However, like many before him who have been summarily strapped into the boardroom ejector seat, Olsen was compassionately fitted with a golden parachute in the shape of a severance payment of roughly a quarter of a million pounds.

The disease reaches a dangerous stage when failure is more liberally rewarded than success, and abject failure becomes the most lucrative goal at which an ambitious manager can aim. Experienced corporate therapists recognize that the symptoms include diminished libido and self-esteem and multiple contusions of the ego. The emollient effect of copious and generous applications of money is, however, well established, to such an extent that this has now become the recommended treatment of first choice.

Accusations of poor judgement can hardly be levelled at managers who pursue the currently fashionable policy of rewarding failure as generously as success. Moreover, sympathetic handling of individual cases of success deficiency has also to be recognized as no more than enlightened self-interest on the part of other managers who may themselves before long fall victim to the same disease.

Motivation Deficiency Disorder

A CLASSIC DEFICIENCY disorder that is largely confined to the ranks of senior management. It provides a rare example of a syndrome with no discernible symptoms; evidence of its existence is provided only by the prophylactic measures that are taken by organizations that wish to be sure of protecting senior staff, and themselves, from its dreadful consequences.

Paradoxically, therefore, proof of the very existence of this widely feared disorder depends entirely on its absence, due to the preventive measures that have now become routine. These include such typical prophylactic strategies as substantial bonuses to reward the achievement of targets. (To eliminate the undesirable risk of not achieving them, the targets are deliberately set at unambitious levels.) There are lavish bonuses also in return for loyalty. Thus, completion of a month or two in office qualifies the manager for shares; and subsequent completion of a full three months will trigger attractive share options (the typical maintenance dose thought necessary to motivate directors is an option to buy at least 2,000 shares at intervals of not longer than three months).

The most subtle of all incentives to turn in outstanding performance comes in the shape of a guarantee of substantial compensation on dismissal.

Penile Dementia

THIS UNFORTUNATE CONDITION (which sometimes gives rise to inappropriate and unseemly mirth) is, basically, a transference to the corporate environment of the malady identified by Freud as 'penis envy'. Victims covet the outward and visible manifestations of size – the tower block erected to house a 'Training Centre', the shiny fleet of limousines, the costly and pretentious 'corporate identity' – and become deeply envious of other organizations which they perceive, rightly or wrongly, as being better endowed than their own. One of the earlier morbid symptoms is often a decision to rechristen the personnel department the 'human resources division'. Renamed, restaffed and re-equipped, this once obscure department embarks on a huge range of imaginative activities that have two things in common. The first is that their value and effectiveness are incapable of measurement, the second is total irrelevance to profit and, indeed, to all the functions that enable a company to make one.

As the condition worsens, the patient becomes more and more preoccupied with phallic symbols. Grave signs include a decision to set up a 'staff college', or to build a new head office.

Gross Cranial Enlargement
(Atlas Syndrome)

A DISTRESSING AFFLICTION in which the physical appearance of the patient soon becomes grossly misshapen. As the limbs, trunk and torso waste away, the head, as if in compensation, swells alarmingly, presenting in time a similar profile to that of Atlas bearing the world on his shoulders.

Two examples of organizations in an advanced stage of the disease may serve to illustrate its ravages.

The Church of England was first diagnosed as a victim when the number of parish churches and, consequently, incumbent priests declined dramatically. Then, in a sequence of developments that is characteristic of the malady, as the numbers of active parish priests collapsed, observers noticed a huge increase in the ranks of diocesan and suffragan bishops, archbishops, archdeacons, canons and other senior functionaries with impressive titles. Burdened with the duty of supporting such a top-heavy apparatus of ecclesiastical bureaucrats, the finances of the Church soon deteriorated into a parlous state, while its demands on the generosity of dwindling congregations became insupportable.

What are commonly known as the Armed Forces offer another example of an organization in the grip of this condition. Again, its remorseless progress follows the classic pattern: a gradual collapse in the numbers of fighting personnel and in the quantities of warlike equipment required for combat is paralleled by a steep rise in the numbers of senior ranks. In the Navy, there will soon be (if there are not already) more admirals than ships; and the number of desks being flown by air marshals considerably exceeds those of aircraft in front-line squadrons.

Counselling Dependence Syndrome

THIS INCREASINGLY COMMON disorder can take either of two forms. In one the victim becomes dependent on *receiving* counselling, while in the second the addiction is to *giving* it.

The typical victim of the first type is an ailing organization so far gone down the precipitous slopes of decline that it is largely incapable of managing its own affairs. The intimate knowledge that its managers possess of the organization, its staff and operations, the years of experience that they have amassed, is suddenly recognized as valueless. The patient loses confidence, becomes hesitant and indecisive, given to hasty, irrational decisions, the commonest of which is to call in management consultants.

Indeed, the growth of management consultancy mirrors and closely parallels the rapid spread of the counselling addiction on which this increasingly lucrative profession has been built. Fortified by a healthy ignorance of the client's operations, and untrammelled by the slightest knowledge of the weaknesses and strengths of those who work for it, the management consultant is in a position to give clients the counselling that they crave and on which they soon become totally dependent.

The addiction, which is enormously expensive, can fast outstrip the resources of its victims, who, in order to fund their craving, are reduced either to begging from shareholders or to desperate attempts to merge with a more prosperous organization.

Whereas some are addicted to being counselled,

others suffer from an addiction to counselling others. Thus the AA (whose members pay a substantial subscription purely in the expectation of swift assistance at the roadside if their cars break down) has become addicted to offering advice in a whole range of unrelated areas.

As the egos of senior managers inflate, they become resentful of the limited role that has hitherto been theirs, and begin to covet a wider stage on which to strut. In no time at all they are offering, unasked, advice on topics such as urban and environmental planning and coming forward, uninvited, with legal and medical advice.

Chairman's Mouth

ALTHOUGH ITS NAME may suggest that this is purely an oral condition, Chairman's Mouth is in fact a disease of the entire corporate communications system. Its onset is characterized by an increasingly stilted, grandiloquent and circumlocutory style of speech and writing, along with an addiction to bizarre euphemisms and orotund phraseology.

The means by which the organization pursues its legitimate goal of survival is referred to as a 'mission'; people become known as 'human resources'; while the legacy of irrational prejudices, obsolete products, ineffective methods, obscure traditions and outmoded working practices is pretentiously described as a 'heritage'. Before long, insoluble problems are described as 'challenges', and crippling setbacks as 'exciting opportunities'.

Hugely contagious, the condition spreads rapidly, infecting first other members of the board, and eventually spreading downwards through the lower ranks of management.

Early Warning Symptoms

FOR THOSE WHO learn to recognize them, there are several unmistakable early warning symptoms of impending corporate collapse. Among the most ominous is a sudden drastic reorganization of the entire corporate structure. One of the best descriptions of this age-old process was written many centuries ago by Petronius: 'I was to learn later in life that we tend to meet any new situation by reorganizing – and a wonderful method it can be for creating the illusion of progress while producing confusion, ineffectiveness and demoralization'.

There are several other tell-tale symptoms of imminent disaster. One of the most reliable is the introduction of meaningless symbols of a corporate solidarity that is largely non-existent (a figment of the board's collective imagination), giving tangible expression to an unholy alliance between the public relations and human resources departments.

A reliable indicator is publication, for internal circulation, of a company journal. Seen by management as a reliable replacement for such traditional, informal and effective methods of communication as gossip in the lavatories, corridors and smoking rooms, these publications are generally viewed with suspicion by most members of the staff on account of their stridently complacent tone. Their pages are devoted to obsequious accounts of management activities, and tend to have the same relentlessly up-beat character of the commentaries on old Gaumont-British and Pathé wartime newsreels. Precluded under threat of instant dismissal from covering topics of genuine interest to their readers, for example salaries, financial and sexual scandals, the editors are obliged to fall back on boringly uncontentious topics approved by senior managers. The scale of news value is bizarre, with speeches by the managing director and the scores of the company darts team accorded automatically the same headline domination that tabloids reserve for royalty and sex.

Even more reliable than the company journal as a symptom of terminal complacency is an attempt by the board to encourage staff to give their loyalty and pride musical expression in the form of a company song, a corporate musical rite that has recently been imported from Japan.

Competitive Dedication Syndrome

MANAGERS WHO HAVE little else to occupy their minds often seek fulfilment in ostentatious competitive displays of dedication to the company. The onset of the neurosis may take a form that seems relatively harmless, such as an early-morning visit to the office of a colleague. Finding him absent, the visitor succumbs to the temptation that is such a characteristic feature of the illness, and seizes the opportunity to demonstrate a superior level of commitment to the company by leaving his colleague a note: 'Need to discuss the revised profit forecast with you urgently'. Thus far, the message is harmless enough. What makes it an unmistakable symptom of competitive neurosis is the triumphant addition to signature and date of the time of the visit ('0700').

The impression that this is intended to give of a manager so committed to the company that he arrives at work before most of his colleagues have even had a shave illustrates the intensely competitive nature of the illness.

Its sinister aspect is that it is highly contagious. The colleague who finds on his desk a message such as this is driven to respond in a way that demonstrates an even higher level of commitment. He will therefore bide his time until late evening when everyone else has left the building, then sneak along to his colleague's office to leave on his desk the reply: 'Sorry not to have been able to reply to your note before. Have been in meetings all day since a working breakfast with PJ. Ready when you are to talk about the forecasts. Roger. 21/9 (2130)'.

When victims of this debilitating syndrome grow weary of advertising in ostentatious ways their increasingly bizarre times of arrival and departure, the competitive neurosis takes a graver turn. Not content with foregoing their holiday entitlement ('far too much to do'; 'just can't spare the time') they next refuse to take time off when ill, insisting on coming to the office to share the virus with colleagues. Only in cases of total physical incapacity do they choose to stay at home, and even then insist on calling colleagues on their bedside mobiles, rather in the manner of people who bid by telephone at auctions.

An extreme example of the way the disorder can affect its victim's sense of values was provided by a manager of my acquaintance who happened to hear on his sick bed news of a terrorist bomb explosion near the office. Instantly he seized the telephone to ask, not 'Has anyone been hurt?' but 'Has the computer been damaged?'

Needless to say, Competitive Dedication Syndrome has appalling consequences for the quality of management decisions which, as the disorder gains a hold, are to an increasing extent taken by people who are stale, exhausted, jet lagged or ill, drained by a life or death struggle with each other to kill the company with dedication.

Rogue Reflex Disorder

A CONDITION IN which the reflex reactions of the patient are conspicuously bizarre, irrelevant or both. It is as if a tap of the padded hammer on the elbow were to produce a convulsive movement of the leg. No manager likes to be seen doing nothing (even when masterly inactivity would be the most appropriate response), especially when strident voices are insisting that 'something must be done'.

Suppose, for example, that the survival of one of our species of bird life is suddenly called into question; numbers are said to have declined alarmingly, to such an extent that the species is seen to be threatened with extinction. The causes of this dramatic decline have been identified as a combination of the indiscriminate use of pesticides, destruction of the hedgerows, and, to a very limited extent, the activities of egg collectors. The normal reflex response would obviously be stricter control of the use of pesticides, along with effective action to preserve the hedgerows. However, both would prove expensive and cause offence to industrial and farming lobbies.

So, for the Rogue Reflex sufferer the greatly preferred course of action would be something ostentatious and bizarre. Something that hits the headlines without hitting anybody's pocket, while attracting approving comment from the media. This might take the form of, firstly, an announcement that certain carefully selected nesting sites would be protected round the clock by heavily armed SAS patrols; and, second, the announcement of an 'egg collectors' amnesty'. For a specified period, collectors would be able to hand in, free of penalty, any eggs in their possession that had been neither stolen nor purchased. In response to a planted question in the House, the Home Secretary would be able gravely to confirm that the amnesty extended to ostrich, turtle and alligator eggs (provided that they had not been traded for profit or human consumption).

Naturally the threatened species would become rapidly extinct, a denouement which the government would vehemently deny, asserting that there was no evidence that the birds had not simply gone into hiding from the hordes of egg collectors who threatened their survival.

This example illustrates the classic course of the disorder; for it is the irrelevance of reaction to stimulus that makes possible a confident differential diagnosis.

Corporate Disintegration Syndrome

THE FIRST STAGE of this terminal malady is marked by the gradual onset of Degenerative Competence Disease. Its visible sign is the loss of skilled and experienced people, due either to retirement or a move to better-paid employment. This trend is often exacerbated by the well-intentioned introduction of job evaluation schemes. Intended to establish some kind of notional parity between holders of jobs which, although in different departments, are considered to be of roughly equal value to the company, these popular human resources schemes have the effect of making it difficult, if not impossible, to give key individuals rewards appropriate to the value of their role and contribution. Precisely what this value is becomes measurable only when an individual leaves the company. The scale of the organization's loss of priceless expertise and skills becomes apparent when successors are appointed, whose resources of ability, experience and talent never match the standard of their predecessors (a phenomenon predicted by the Law of Decadent Succession which decrees that managers promoted to a job are always of inferior calibre to the previous incumbent.)

Nevertheless, inferior or not, the manager just promoted to what has always been seen as a key post immediately acquires the status of an expert, together with a notional market value considered appropriate to his new position. As a result he is likely after only a short while in the post to be approached with an offer of a better-paid position, leaving vacant a post which will soon (in accordance with the Law explained above) be filled by an even more inferior replacement.

To this inexorable process of degeneration, the human resources department makes its own distinctive contribution: first, by insisting on a policy of promoting from within, thus significantly narrowing the field from which replacements can be chosen; and, second, by ensuring that none of the numerous training programmes that it sponsors relates in any way to the technical performance of specific jobs. In accordance with time-honoured human resources practice, all training courses deal with such airy generalities as 'communication skills' and 'personal development'. This lack of any specific technical focus for their training guarantees steadily declining standards of technical performance by the staff.

The factors just mentioned combine to produce another familiar corporate phenomenon: the Spiral of Accelerating Desperation, as senior management feverishly strives to find in the organization people to promote into the vacant jobs.

A case history may help to illustrate the typical course of the disorder. Imagine, for a moment, that the stricken company is engaged in the conjuring business. Due to dismissals, departures and retirement the shortage of people with conjuring skills becomes suddenly acute; bookings are cancelled and engagements have to be refused. To fill the vacancies, junior accounts clerks are hurriedly promoted to the rank of conjuror, and secretaries made up to senior illusionists. While no one is actually taught to pull a rabbit from a hat or saw a woman in half, much time is spent in meetings discussing the type of silk to be used in the manufacture of top hats, the quality of wood from which the coffin of the woman to be sawn in half is made, and the precise specification of the saw. For good measure, the human resources people contribute helpful courses on 'The Role of Illusion in Management', and 'Personal Development for Junior Magicians'.

However, despite these well-meant efforts, the disease continues to take its inevitable course. A grave sign comes when senior management collectively develop the malady known as Collaborative Comfort Fantasy. This takes the form of an irrational refusal to face up to the reality of the company's position. Despite a disastrous fall in profits, declining attendances and a slump in bookings, managers collude to put a brave face on the company's plight, acting, for all the world, as if it were in rude health. Promotions continue to be made ('pleased to announce the appointment'), mellifluous proclamations issued ('Join me in congratulating Roger on his new advancement and in wishing him well in dealing with the challenges that face us').

Finally, as the seas of disaster close over the company's head, the only signs left of the existence of a once prosperous firm are the bubbles still rising to the surface from now submarine management babble ('To take advantage of the new opportunities presented by receivership, I have appointed Rupert . . .').

Pangloss Disease

A DISORDER TO which politicians and managers are particularly prone, Pangloss is a chronic condition of which the salient presenting symptom is an extraordinary, indeed, pathological complacency. Sufferers develop a blinkered view of the world that renders them incapable of recognizing any trend, development or event that might tend to damage the individual's complacent conviction that (in the words of Voltaire's famous character) 'all is for the best in the best of all possible worlds'.

The disease is easiest to diagnose at party conferences and the kind of corporate gatherings where staff or shareholders assemble to hear a progress report from the chief executive. Unimpressive or disappointing results are described as a 'tribute to the efforts of our dedicated staff' – in reality, a motley crew of indolent second-raters whom the Pangloss victim, nevertheless, is likely to describe as 'the team of brilliantly talented people whom we are lucky to employ'. The range of shoddy and overpriced products marketed by the company are referred to proudly as the 'first-rate products of a unique fusion of world class design and state-of-the-art technology'.

Typical Pangloss sufferers tend to associate exclusively with other victims, and within their own organizations promote subordinates who bring them glad tidings, while punishing ruthlessly those who bring bad news. As a result the disease becomes endogenous, and leads inexorably to the organization's demise.

Stupor Conventii (Delegates' Disease)

OUTBREAKS OF 'DELEGATES' Disease' (as this malady is also known) are common at such corporate gatherings as meetings, conferences, presentations and conventions, where, unless action is taken rapidly, the disease (which is highly contagious) spreads like the proverbial wildfire.

The first symptom to manifest itself is a sensation of weight in the eyelids, which soon begin to droop uncontrollably. The victim's breathing becomes slow and stertorous; at the same time the muscles of the neck become progressively less adequate to the role of supporting the head, which sags helplessly towards the victim's chest. Sufferers find it more and more difficult to concentrate, and attempts to follow a presentation become increasingly fitful and laboured; the succession of slides projected onto a brightly lit screen exerts a powerfully hypnotic, soporific influence on the stricken audience. A common symptom is the sensation that psychologists know as 'déjà vu', a feeling that all the facts and figures in a presentation have been heard before, and that the words and statistics on the slides simply repeat those already articulated by the speaker.

Without swift remedial action in the shape of oxygen and stimulants (taken orally), preferably accompanied by immediate replacement of the speaker, and a change of subject, the sufferer lapses into a kind of narcoleptic state from which he can only be aroused with the greatest difficulty.

Compulsive Prognosis Disorder

THIS DISEASE IS an aberrant form of the age-old human longing to see into the future. As the name suggests, it takes the form of a compulsive drive to issue forecasts. In affected organizations, where the disease soon becomes endemic, forecasting meetings are held at more and more frequent intervals. As the disease takes hold, forecasting becomes an activity in its own right and the resulting forecasts acquire the status of a major product line. The forecasts themselves bear little relation to eventual results, and, in an effort to narrow the gap between forecast and achievement, a whole hierarchy of forecasts emerges – original forecasts, decision forecasts, revised forecasts and so on through a succession of revisions.

The managers of afflicted companies derive from the forecasting process the gratification that more rational organizations extract from actual achievement. Thus, when the forecast submitted is deemed inadequate or too conservative, the figures are adjusted upwards. The higher profit and lower expenditure figures submitted in the place of those so contemptuously rejected, give everyone concerned a glow of satisfaction that is hardly diminished at all by the failure (which only emerges much later) to achieve results that come anywhere near the optimistic forecasts.

In the terminal stages of this illness more time is occupied making forecasts and producing plans than in the various activities conducive to achieving them.

Obsessional Status Neurosis

RATHER AS MEMBERS of the acting profession devote much energy and time to ceremonies at which statuettes, shields and other trophies are awarded to selected luvvies, managers too develop a morbid appetite for status. While doing a job well might be thought to confer a certain status on the holder, it has the disadvantage of being dependent on performance. More coveted therefore are titles which, as Lord Melbourne observed of the Order of the Garter, involve 'no damned nonsense about merit'.

The range of such titles is extensive, including as it does not only President, Chairman, Executive Chairman, Chief Executive and Director, but also such junior accolades as Associate Director, Senior Associate Director, Vice President and Senior Vice President. (Some organizations have as many subtle hierarchical gradations as the Royal Victorian Order, with its Knights Grand Cross, Knights Commander, Companions and Members.)

Though the titles themselves afford much simple pleasure, this is all the keener when other tangible tokens of status are attached to them – such as size or situation of office, type, colour and surface area of desk or carpet, make and cubic capacity of car and similar visible symbols of status that other people can envy.

In extreme forms of the condition, titles will often be accepted in lieu of financial reward.

Impotence

THE PREVALENCE OF this distressing condition is in large part due to sufferers' reluctance to seek professional advice. In consequence, some unfortunate victims undergo years of needless suffering before in desperation they find someone able to help them.

The condition manifests itself as an inability on the part of management to recognize that there are some problems to which no purely administrative solution can ever be found. Usually this happens when the problem is basically one of *selection*, not administration. No matter how the cards are shuffled, or how many times the organization chart has to be redrawn, the inconvenient fact remains that the composition of the pack remains unaltered, and that it is in precisely this fact that the problem has it roots. Much time and energy is devoted to a doomed attempt to find an administrative answer to a qualitative problem.

The first step towards a cure is taken when the sufferer can be brought to accept the intractable nature of his problem, when he is persuaded to abandon the fruitless pursuit of administrative answers, and made to face the unwelcome fact that his problem will only be solved when he can bring himself to hire one or two really good people and put them in key jobs.

When this happens, relief can be both swift and dramatic. Their lives transformed by acceptance of the limitations of administrative tinkering, managements feel liberated from the inhibitions imposed by human resources dogma and various forms of managerial and political correctness. Casting aside the emasculating influence of policies on 'promotion from within', seminars on the 'Role of the Manager', and 'Management of Change', along with all the other impedimenta forced upon them by ambitious human resources personnel, they feel at last 'empowered' simply to hire the best and fire the worst people for the jobs.

Reduced Consciousness Syndrome

THIS SYNDROME, WHICH long escaped recognition, has only recently become apparent with the emergence of 'awareness' events. These have included 'Menopause Awareness Week', the 'Condom Awareness' campaign, and, most recently, South Eastern Water's imaginative and hugely successful 'Water Awareness' campaign. This brought to the attention of a hitherto unconscious public the existence, characteristics and benefits of water, a natural commodity whose ubiquitous familiarity had resulted in many people not only taking it for granted, but also overlooking its potential for such arcane purposes as bathing, washing, drinking and even flushing toilets.

Victims exist in a state which, although falling some way short of true and total unconsciousness, is thought to render them partially oblivious of the people and objects that surround them. It is indeed a form of cataleptic state that will be familiar to anyone who comes in frequent contact with railway staff, or who attempts to get served at the cosmetics counter of a department store.

As will be seen from the description above, the syndrome can be difficult to diagnose; its presence is most commonly deduced from the remedy prescribed. There is however little doubt that Reduced Consciousness Syndrome is as much a disease of management as it is of society as a whole, calling for energetic prophylactic measures designed to raise management consciousness of risks and opportunities to at least the level found in hibernating bats.

Panic Attacks

AN INCREASINGLY COMMON malady of management is a tendency to repeated attacks of blind panic. Victims are gripped by a sense of dread and impending doom which is nonetheless distressing for being quite irrational. The cause is usually one of the sudden down turns in profit which are an inevitable feature of the business cycle, but which few corporate managements are able to accept with equanimity. As a result, massive overreaction is the usual response to the problem.

Seizures of panic affect the judgement of the patient, whose dread of criticism by City analysts and columnists results in increasingly frantic attempts to produce a short-term cosmetic improvement to the balance sheet, usually at the expense of long-term health. Staff emoluments are slashed, causing many of the best to leave. Savage cutbacks are ordered of the firm's more costly operations, which usually turn out to be those that make the biggest profits.

Typically, symptoms include entry to the corporate vocabulary of such terms as 'down-sizing', 'out-sourcing', and ' restructuring' – all euphemistic terms for the panic-stricken dismissal of large numbers of employees. Before long the organization falls victim to a vicious circle initiated by the fact that the first to be dismissed are usually older employees who are generally among the few members of staff who have the experience and knowledge needed to rescue their employer. Their dismissal produces illusory savings which seldom exceed in size the cost of engaging replacements, which, when added to the cost of redundancy payments, results more often in additions than in reductions to the costs of operation. As a result the corporation sinks into further decline which at some point may become irreversible.

Canute's Disease

A MALADY THAT is only too familiar to political observers and students of morbid management, Canute's Disease, as the name suggests, manifests itself as a total inability to accept or recognize reality. It is characterized by blind obduracy and obtuseness, two qualities that sufferers imagine will be mistaken for resolution and courage. The disease in time produces in the victim a compulsive repetition of certain words and phrases, along with other repetitive patterns of speech that signal the affliction as clearly as adolescent spots reveal the presence of acne. 'We shall win decisively; we shall win convincingly; we shall win dramatically!' is, for example, the kind of repetitive mantra favoured by a party leader who faces defeat at a general election. The expression 'peace process' is another manifestation of Canute's Disease, mouthed obsessively by politicians rendered unable by the disease to recognize reality, even when their babblings of peace are being drowned by the sound of bombs exploding.

Compulsive Calling Disorder

CHARACTERIZED BY DELUSIONS of competence in unrelated fields, Compulsive Calling Disorder is a socially transmitted disease. The most obvious symptom is a compulsive urge to offer a copious flow of advice on matters of which the sufferer is unqualified to speak. It is a disorder to which employers' organizations and trade unions are particularly prone. Their compulsive urge to offer counsel uninvited produces, prior to a Budget, a flood of fiscal and economic advice from such organizations as the CBI, the TUC and the Institute of Directors.

Since much of this advice predictably conflicts in a way that reflects the prevalent concerns of each, all of it can safely be ignored.

Unaccountably, trade unions seem to imagine that their advice will be particularly valued on issues of which they have no experience, and in areas where they lack any direct responsibility, competence or interest, such, for example, as the laws that govern applications for political sanctuary in Britain. The BMA too, whose functions at no point impinge on law enforcement or the subject's liberties, feels inexplicably impelled to issue a call for motorists to be breathalysed at random. For some reason this meddlesome advice is usually described as a 'call' or a 'demand'.

Thus, at the height of the calling season teachers' unions will be making medical demands, while the health service union calls for changes in education and foreign policy.

Multiple Accreditation Disorder

SKILLED DIAGNOSTICIANS QUICKLY learn to spot the tell-tale symptoms of this curious disorder. These are noticeable first in the company's reception area where the walls are seen to be generously plastered with framed documents, each bearing the impressive seal and logo of some little-known organization that issues, in exchange for a substantial fee, a certificate attesting to the fact that the company named thereon has 'satisfied its standards'.

This assemblage of testimonials from organizations whose sole business transaction with the accredited firm has been to pocket some of its money, and whose opinion of its standards of probity, competence, quality, training (or whatever) is therefore untainted by any personal experience of its services or products, is thought to be of real commercial value. Companies fear that, if they decided to forego the prestige believed to attach to a display of accreditation logos on their premises and letterheads, they would be in danger of losing business to competitors more liberally endowed with these largely meaningless symbols. A critical stage of the disorder is reached when sufferers begin to make a larger investment in gaining seals of approval than they do in winning customers.

False Achievement Syndrome

THE SYNDROME IS far from being exclusively a disorder of the body corporate. Individuals, too, are subject to a morbid attachment to the symbols of achievement, which soon become accepted as substitutes for the actual attainment of objectives. Thus, people who long to lose weight without making the sacrifices involved in reducing their consumption of alcohol or food, and in taking a lot more exercise, make a substantial investment in some costly piece of equipment that is widely recognized as a means of achieving the goal they have announced, such, for example, as a rowing machine or a captive bicycle. Over a relatively short period of time this, so to speak, physical declaration of intent becomes a substitute for the desired achievement; its installation in the patient's home or office is a pleasant substitute for losing weight. Before long the sufferer begins to believe that by buying the equipment he has actually lost weight – a classic case of False Achievement Syndrome.

In the corporate sector, too, a really substantial investment in the means of reaching some objective soon becomes mistaken by management for the achievement itself: an expensive new computer system, a radical reshuffle of jobs, a costly relocation to new premises, a huge down-sizing operation; the investment is often all management needs to form the false conviction that the ostensible objectives have been triumphantly achieved.

Laws of Management

The Law of Extravagant Economy

Economy measures usually cost more than the sum total of savings achieved

WE HAVE ALL come across them: nit-picking, chicken-shit (to borrow a blunt turn of phrase from Lyndon Johnson, who once rebuked a journalist by contemptuously snorting 'you've a goddam nerve to come to the President of the United States and ask a chickenshit question like that!') economy measures, many entirely symbolic, portentously announced, and implemented with a fanatical zeal that their value to the organization seldom justifies.

In my time I have witnessed economy 'initiatives' that range from the embarrassing to the bizarre. One company made a small saving on its Buildings and Contents insurance by prohibiting personal kettles (which are supposed to represent a small extra risk of fire). The minuscule saving achieved was rapidly outweighed by the cost of time lost to the firm by employees who, denied their private brews, soon fell into the habit of slipping out to tea and coffee bars.

Another firm kept in its stationery store a stock of paper tissues. These were obtainable, free, by any member of the staff who needed them to mop up tea, nosebleeds, dripping noses or deal with other minor problems of corporate liquidity. The cost of providing this small but welcome service could only have been minimal, but the goodwill generated by this modest perk was far from negligible. Consequently, its withdrawal by some beady-eyed accountant was greatly resented. The company earned, instead of respect for prudent housekeeping, nothing but disdain for what was widely seen as parsimony. 'Mean as shithouse rats' was the universal verdict.

Another favourite target of managers looking for ways to save money is the office telephone, in particular out-going calls. Some organizations treat staff considered reliable enough to hold responsible jobs as if, in the matter of telephone usage, they were likely to behave like disaffected servants, incessantly making protracted, long-distance calls at their employers' expense. The petty restrictions often placed on private calls made from the office not only cause resentment; they actually discourage staff from working by obliging them to spend time away from their desks as they go out in search of a public telephone in working order.

Companies that ignore the Law of Extravagant Economy often pay a heavy price: the reputation of being 'a good company to work for', is won with difficulty but quickly and easily lost.

The Law of Proportional Incompetence

*The proportion of incompetent to able people is the
same in all walks of life*

A POPULAR MISCONCEPTION is that practitioners' abilities increase in proportion to the duration of their
training. Thus, it is widely believed that, for example,
there are more incompetent plumbers than accountants,
or that the proportion of grossly incompetent people is
certain to be higher in the teaching than in the medical
profession.

The fact is, however, that egregious incompetence
(inefficiency and ineptitude on a truly epic scale) is
evenly distributed throughout the whole working population. It is, unhappily, only later in life that the majority of people grasp the full awesome implications of the
Law. For it means, *inter alia*, that each of us is as likely
to be bankrupted by a lawyer or accountant as we are to
be flooded by the actions of a plumber or made home-
less by a builder, as liable to be the victim of ill health
caused by doctors as of a disastrous fire brought about
by the incompetence of an electrician.

The often misplaced trust that 'professionals'
command represents a triumph of hope and tradition
over actual experience.

The Law of Collusive Preferment

A company's health can be judged by the size of its board

COMPANIES THAT ARE doing well seem able to manage with only a small number of directors. Once they run into trouble, however, it is usually not long before a leaf or two needs to be added to the boardroom table. An extended table is required to seat extra directors, newly appointed to the board in order that the blame for failure may be more widely shared, being thought too heavy a burden to be carried by the original few.

The Law of Collusive Preferment has profound implications for shareholders, staff and members of the wider public. It means that the sudden appointment to a board of several new directors is an early warning sign of trouble – a signal that it might be as well to sell your shares, leave to join another firm, or transfer your custom elsewhere. The burden of financing incentives for all the new directors may well prove to be the last straw.

The Law of Progressive Regression

Automation means frustration

WHAT IS THE dominant sound to be heard in any supermarket? The eerie beep of the bar code machines, music to the ears of management, a veritable futuristic symphony of trade. To most customers, however, the music would be sweeter if the machine would only read their packages first time. How often have you had to stand there, fuming, while the operator passes the same pack again and again across the window, which refuses obstinately to record your purchase? Getting out of shops which have bar code readers is like trying to enter the USA without the essential visa in your passport.

It was easier and quicker in the old days when, free of all the delays inseparable from automation, the girl on the till just totted up the prices on the packets. Since few school-leavers today seem able to add up in their heads, the simple sums involved have to be done for them by machines, with all the delays that sophisticated technology involves. Brains have now been replaced by pocket calculators. (I was once kept waiting in a shop while the girl who took the money had to use her machine to calculate the sum of £3.50, £8 and £10. Frowning, tongue protruding from her lips in concentration, she took twice as long to punch the calculator buttons as it would have taken an 8-year-old to do the sum in its head.)

Another regressive application of technology is the telephone answering system that invites you to make contact with the appropriate department by punching digits on your telephone: 'Punch 5 if you have a billing enquiry. If you have a query about our service, punch 2. Punch 3 if you wish to place an order. Punch 6 to make a payment.' Delivered by a female voice with the exaggerated elocution of a patronizing governess speaking to a backward child, such messages take up a great deal of valuable time. Moreover, the one omission from many of these 'menus' is the most probable reason you have for making the call in the first place, which is to make a complaint.

No less harmful to the caller's blood pressure is another development in telephonic customer relations: this is the ability to fill what might otherwise be an awkward and protracted silence with repetitious snatches of muzak, alternating with what are doubtless intended to be words of reassurance: 'Your call is being held in a queue' ... 'Your place in the queue is being maintained' ... 'Thank you for calling; your call is still held in a queue'. A discernible by-product of the Law is that the longer it takes for a live voice to come on the line, the more urgent and lively the tempo of the music you are made to listen to while waiting.

Eventually the organization becomes increasingly isolated and withdrawn, and develops an irrational fear of the outside world. Shunning all forms of direct human contact, it retreats into a world of its own, insulated by electronics from intrusive callers.

The Law of Posterior Deference

Respect attaches to the chair, not the occupant

THE PIVOTAL ROLE played in corporate life by the buttocks is reflected in the vocabulary of management. The individual running a meeting is addressed and referred to as the 'chair'. Those seen as over-anxious to ingratiate themselves with superiors are described as 'brown-nosed', while those who have been heavily criticized by a superior are said to have been 'crapped on'.

Rather as is the case with baboons, whose striking scarlet behinds are displayed as a deferential gesture of submission, the manager's buttocks play a significant role in determining status. The difference is that in Corporate Man the buttocks are deployed as a means of securing deference from others. It is also considered more appropriate and seemly to transfer the submission and respect due to managers from the buttocks themselves to the seat in which they are regularly lodged, which becomes a kind of surrogate posterior, a symbol of authority, wisdom and status.

This can be clearly seen whenever (as frequently happens) a manager who has been widely perceived as able and effective is replaced by someone who is conspicuously deficient in ability, intelligence or talent. Because deference flows towards and attaches to the seat, the newly enstooled occupant (who may well have hitherto been widely regarded as a booby) will instantly, automatically inherit the respect accorded to its previous occupant. No matter how fatuous his suggestions or foolish his decisions, the new incumbent is assured of a respectful and compliant audience solely by virtue of the seat he occupies.

The Law of Remedial Exacerbation

Treatment does more harm than the disorder

IT IS NOW accepted that a prime cause of ill health is the treatment that doctors prescribe. This type of illness is known to doctors as 'iatrogenic', a title sufficiently opaque to conceal from inquisitive laymen the nature of their illness.

In the same way, corporate failure and decline can often be traced to the well-intentioned measures that management has taken, usually on the recommendation of plausible consultants. Most of the realistic remedial measures open to a company are so obvious that even the incumbent management could think of them unaided. Consultants therefore need to come up with prescriptions that are radical enough to justify the substantial bill that they will eventually present. In consequence, their recommendations usually tend to involve ingenious and complex restructuring measures which, when duly implemented, have the predictable effect of causing chaos, as staff struggle manfully to cope with new and different working practices.

Take, for example, the case of a firm engaged in the mail order business which called in management consultants to come up with a prescription for making its promotion department more profitable, efficient and productive. (On all three counts its recent performance was thought to have been flagging.)

Before coming up with their recommendations, the consultants devoted several weeks to a careful examination of the promotion department, its functions, objectives and working practices, and the way it related to other departments of the company. They concluded (correctly) that the largest share of the company's profits was directly attributable to this department's operations. They also concluded (again quite correctly) that the department's health was crucially dependent on a flow of good ideas. They noted that, historically, most of the good ideas had come from creative people employed as writers or designers. What was missing, they explained, was a *system* that could be relied on for a steady and copious supply of good ideas.

The prescription they came up with was to set up what the consultants described as a 'think tank', a small team of creative people whose function would be to come up with good ideas. At frequent intervals the people who made up the think tank would be changed; this, it was explained, would ensure that the think tank's occupants did not have time to grow stale, and would guarantee plenty of fresh thinking and, therefore, good ideas.

When the consultants presented their proposals to the board, their clients were delighted with what appeared to be a magic formula for producing good ideas, not on the hitherto untidy and unpredictable basis, but in a regular, *disciplined* way. The new system looked set to be what they had always wanted – a kind of industrial alchemist's stone, a method of ensuring that their flock of captive geese would provide a predictable supply of golden eggs. The fee that the consultants charged for their advice was, of course, colossal. And the board concluded that any advice that cost so much was certain to be good. So at first they were happy to dismiss as 'teething problems' the think tank's early failure to come up with good ideas. Indeed, for a long time (certainly far beyond any plausible period of teething problems) they were disinclined to face up to the obvious fact that the think tank was not producing even as many good ideas as the old haphazard system. What, they asked each other with increasing desperation, could possibly have gone wrong with the consultants' costly cure?

The answer (which, at first, they simply refused to accept) provides an object lesson in the terrible risks that are run by managers who dwell in a world of virtual reality.

The consultants' system failed for a simple and obvious reason: the incidence of good ideas is always unpredictable and random. They arrive unplanned, unheralded and unexpectedly. To produce them to order or on schedule is in fact an impossibility – a truth that any junior creative person would have been happy to explain. Anyone with a little more experience could have told them something else: people are creative in different ways. Very few are capable of coming up with new ideas; the majority depend for survival on picking the brains of a few inventive individuals.

It can therefore be seen that the think tank, with its constantly changing complement of people, was as good a way as any of ensuring a *reduction* in the flow of good ideas. For most of the time, the few individuals capable of having them were deprived of all responsibility for producing them, and, indeed, excluded from the process of creating them.

This typical example of iatrogenic disorder illustrates just how easily the cure can prove to be more damaging than the malady itself.

The Law of Delegated Culpability

The fault is always someone else's

ONE OF THE prime qualifications for success in management is the ability to delegate responsibility. Asked to name areas of responsibility that they consider suitable for delegation, most managers would think first of failure. Enlightened management makes use of a whole range of sophisticated methods for delegating culpability to others.

Hostage Management (q.v.) and, of course, committees are among the methods most often used to delegate. 'It's your decision old boy!' the senior manager exclaims, slipping an avuncular arm around the shoulders of a colleague. Anyone naive enough to accept the invitation can be sure of getting all the blame for a disaster. Nor should he expect to get much of the credit should the decision turn out to be a good one. His senior colleague will let it be known that the decision was taken principally on his advice. An even more refined technique is refusing to take a decision at all, in the hope that someone – anyone – else will eventually be driven by exasperation or impatience to put his head on the block.

The Law of Experimental Elevation

Promotion is the only conclusive means of establishing incapacity

WHAT PEOPLE ARE incapable of doing is something that can only be established conclusively by asking them to do it. From this it follows that, in the hands of an enlightened management, promotion can be used as a precision instrument for detecting what members of staff are incapable of doing. It will also be seen that employees who are still performing well, doing their jobs with reasonable competence and skill, have yet to achieve their full potential for promotion. In ensuring that they do finally achieve it, the company's job evaluation scheme plays a significant role.

Take for example a salesman whose agreeable manner, persuasive tongue and knowledge of its products, to say nothing of his understanding of the customers, contribute substantially to the company's profits. In due course its job evaluation scheme, in which a salary ceiling is laid down for every job, makes it impossible to pay this valuable member of staff anything like what he has been worth as a salesman.

The only form of career advancement now open to the accomplished salesman is promotion to a more 'important', 'responsible' job. Since every manager's self-esteem depends on the belief that management is the most important of all functions, the successful salesman is promoted to 'sales manager' a role in which the work he is good at, namely, management of sales, is replaced by the management of salesmen, a job that calls for different skills. If, against all odds, he is successful in the role, there is bound to come a time when the Law of Experimental Elevation puts him on the board as 'sales director', a role in which he is almost certain to be a complete disaster. The Law being irreversible, he cannot be demoted, having achieved, experimentally, his full potential for promotion.

The Law of Obsequious Periphrasis

*Advertisements of 'situations vacant' are written
mainly to massage the advertiser's ego*

THERE WAS A time when 'situations vacant' ads were
written by somebody in the firm with a vacancy to
fill, someone who understood the job, and the qualities
required to do it adequately.

These days, because of the prevalence of Abdication
Management (q.v.), the task of recruiting staff tends to
be given to 'experts' in the shape of recruitment consultants. As a direct result of this third party involvement,
the nature of these advertisements has radically altered.
Whereas once, when written by someone in the firm,
they tended to focus sharply on the nature of the job,
and the qualities required of applicants, the recruitment
consultants who now produce them are preoccupied
with making the client feel good. In consequence, most
of the ads are devoted to shameless flattery. The consultants' priority is to keep the client happy, and to this end
much space is devoted to glowing descriptions of the
company, its undisputed position as a market-leader, its
towering stature, unrivalled achievements and laudable
ambitions.

Such fulsome descriptions of the company don't just
make the client feel good, but also help to cement his
relationship with the consultant. And, for good
measure, they also enable the consultants to conceal
their inability to understand the nature of the job and
the qualities required of the individual who gets it.

Here are three examples of this genre. (Although you may find this hard to believe, they are not malicious parodies, but verbatim quotes from recent 'situations vacant' ads.)

In addition to delivering cost effective solutions to the business requirements of DERA, the Facilities Management expertise of DSSD is in increasing demand from major organizations in both private and public sectors.

With a mission to capitalize on the commercial potential of our services whilst maintaining first class support to DERA, we are now in the process of privatizing DSSD and gearing it up to become one of the premier FM providers.

A predominant world player in transportation equipment within an international company, this newly restructured management team is making major inroads into the introduction of modern manufacturing systems to a prestige reputation product, the production of which is now undergoing step changes in a world class competitiveness drive.

Reporting direct to the Operations Director you will direct a shortly to be assembled team of 30 manufacturing engineers amongst a workforce of 1500 and be responsible for leading the attack on process, Kaizen, manufacturing cost-down, concurrent engineering and Economic Value Added initiatives on both present and future product manufacturability. You will be able to hit the floor running in terms of your gravitas, leadership and ability to sell and introduce change, and will have the appropriate professional qualifications combined with a demonstrable record of achievement in a pedigree organization that has achieved performance break-throughs.

Gartner Group is the worldwide leader among IT advi-sory service companies, providing research, analysis and consulting advice on IT strategies for users, purchasers and vendors of IT products and services. Gartner Group has more than 23,000 individual clients, representing more than 1500 associates in 40 countries.

Reporting to the CIO of Gartner Group worldwide, this position is responsible for managing the 15 strong European IS&T organization, including local applica-tions development, telecommunications, end user support and training and management of LAN's and network servers. The VP will assist the CIO in the development of worldwide IS&T strategies and budgets, but, above all, will be responsible for the provision of an excellent service to around 500 Gartner Group users across Europe.

These unctuous, obsequious slabs of deferential prose provide examples of just about every vice known to a student of grammar. For anyone who was at school in the days when English grammar still used to be on the syllabus, they provide a rich source of examples of tautology, hyperbole, oxymoron, split infinitives and other forms of fractured syntax.

The Law of Expectant Valuation

*Anticipated performance is always better rewarded
than achievement*

THERE IS ONE situation in which even the meanest
employer will willingly open his purse and give
freely of its contents. This is when he is about to hire a
new employee whose future contribution is expected to
be large. Note the word 'expected': managers are
forward-looking people, always more grateful for what
they imagine they are about to receive than for what
they have already been given. This is why the most
generous rewards are reserved for expectations rather
than achievements.

Thus the individual brought in to fill a job that has
just fallen vacant will always be paid more than the
previous incumbent. And if the job is a new creation, the
remuneration will be fixed at a significantly higher level
than most of the salaries earned by employees whose
contribution to profits has been demonstrable and
substantial.

A newly hired manager is the beneficiary of the
corporate mutation of a process that is summarized in a
wealth of proverbs about the grass being greener on the
other side, and the superiority of hopeful travel to
arrival.

You will never be in a position to strike a better
bargain with your employer than when you are offered
the job.

The Law of Replicated Triumphs

Attempts by management to replicate triumphs are usually disasters

To REPEAT EARLY triumphs is the aim of most chief executives. Managers have an understandable affection for the stratagems, methods and systems that won them acclaim earlier in their careers. What they tend to forget is that some of the decisions which won them such success may well be inappropriate to their new environment.

One company of my acquaintance achieved worldwide pre-eminence in the specialized world of mail order, a field in which it had built up unrivalled expertise and skills, and which, carefully nurtured by managers promoted from within, continued to bring the organization exponential growth. Then came the day when the company recruited as chief executive a manager whose entire career had been spent in the totally different sphere of entertainment.

In no time at all the new broom had taken two radical decisions. He persuaded the board to forecast (in a notoriously cyclical business) unprecedented, steady growth. At the same time he took a decision that was to make even modest growth virtually impossible. This was done by shedding most of the people whose experience and skills had built the company.

The second decision was to move the organization away from the field of mail order (of which the new man knew very little) towards the entertainment sector in which his reputation had been made. Canny old sweats

114

who understood mail order were replaced by feisty young executives whose pony-tails, earrings and nose jewels testified to their entertainment background.

Not surprisingly, profits slumped, results fell way short of target; staff who had been made redundant departed by the coach load. Another attempt to replicate triumph had ended in disaster.

The Law of Transcendent Methodology

Means soon become more important than ends

IN MOST ORGANIZATIONS the achievement of targets and execution of the 'mission' soon take second place to the means by which these objectives are pursued. The quality of those engaged on pursuing the objectives, and their standards of performance, rapidly become subordinated to the structural framework within which they operate. Organization charts are laboriously drawn up, on which people are shuffled around from one box to another (with the titles of the functions they perform soon replacing the names of the individuals concerned); vertical and horizontal lines are redrawn in ever more complicated patterns, some of which soon come to resemble the wiring diagram for Concorde. Although lip-service is paid to the achievement of ostensible objectives, management's real satisfaction is derived from manipulating structures and procedures. Various committees and subcommittees form, regroup and dissolve in ways reminiscent of amoeba in a laboratory dish.

Few managers are sufficiently clear-sighted and single-minded to keep an eye sharply focused on the ball. Most are happier scrutinizing the rules of the game, the clothes worn by the players, or the venue of the match. This gives rise to a certain imbalance between the attention that is paid to actually achieving their objectives and the means by which they are pursued. The objectives are, let us say, to turn out superior products which are then sold in large quantities to make substantial profits from customers satisfied enough to keep coming back for more.

Clear-cut objectives, you might think, not easily obscured by the way in which the core functions of design, production, sales and what it is now fashionable to describe as 'customer care' carry out their responsibilities.

If that is what you think, you have failed to take into account the relentless way in which application of the Law will produce any number of ways to complicate the process that makes it all too easy to lose sight of the objectives.

Let's start with product selection and design. Here, it would of course be a quite unacceptable risk to rely on judgement, experience and flair. What is needed in order to eliminate risk is some market research.

What form, then, should this take: street interviews, a few focus groups (half a dozen diffident dummies too cowed to disagree with opinions voiced by a single loudmouth with a dominant personality, thus ensuring that each group constitutes what is, in effect, a sample of one?), hall-tests, where randomly chosen people of the target age-group are invited to come in off the street, and look at the items on display? Or, less expensive, a postal questionnaire?

Selection of the appropriate method, a subject of heated debate, is bound to occupy many working hours, while execution of the final choice(s) will be time-consuming and costly. So already we have managed to spend a sizeable amount before even choosing a product.

But suppose that a choice has at last been made, and agreement finally reached on its production. Isn't it now just a question of pressing buttons on production lines, and getting the product out of the factory and into the shops?

Hold on a minute, Roger, not so fast old chap. First of all, where is the factory to be located? How many shall we employ? OK, lets say fifty (and that's just the personnel department). How many colour options shall we offer, and what quantities of each? Best to set up a study group or two and maybe a working party. What about establishing a colour-co-ordination task force and a factory location steering group?

And so, of course, it will go on at each stage of the project; thousands, if not tens of thousands, spent, and not a single widget or gizmo sold, or even made. The only thing to have left the drawing board so far is an organization chart. And there are still several stages to go before our widget appears in the shops, let alone before the original optimistic sales forecast has gone through the subsequent stages of production forecast and revised profit forecast.

This piece itself is an example of the Law in action: the aim, which was simply to help you understand it, has been overtaken by the weight of explanation.

The Law of Subsidiary Inheritance

Subsidiaries inherit the problems of parent companies

SUCH IS THE relationship between them that anything the parent company finds a problem is automatically passed on to the subsidiary, along with whatever in the way of a solution the parent may have found. The adoption of this solution is likely to be mandatory, even, as is often the case with global companies, when the subsidiary finds it useless for the simple reason that it doesn't have the same problem, operating as it does in another country within a different legal and administrative framework.

It is in precisely this kind of situation that Management Fictions (q.v.) can be so helpful. In order to compel a reluctant subsidiary to adopt the parent's solution to a problem that it doesn't have, the parent will issue a global policy instruction based on the fiction that anything which the parent finds a problem is bound to cause the same concern to all the companies it owns.

Thus, for example, the US parent's insistence that safety helmets should be worn at all times throughout the workplace, is enforced with the same zeal in the British company which manufactures paper hats, as in America where the parent company makes steel girders. Failure to apply the same rules to its global workforce would be condemned as bad parenting by the human resources department.

The Law of Rhetorical Divergence

Reality and rhetoric pursue divergent courses

W HEN THE CHIEF executive gives a pep talk, or circulates a memo, it is wise to bear in mind that things are seldom as the management would have you believe them to be. The 'challenges' of which he speaks are likely to be more in the nature of threats to survival. The 'opportunities' that you and your colleagues are adjured to seize and even embrace are what a dispassionate observer might be more inclined to see as insoluble problems. As for the 'restructuring' process in which he has such confidence, you probably know it better as the recent panic dismissal of one third of the workforce.

But for as long as your own job survives the holocaust, you will be privileged to 'work towards our common goal', described in the company's mission statement as 'a partnership between customers, shareholders and employees in which the benefits of sound management and unimpeachable business ethics can be shared equally by all, and ultimately spread beyond our own corporate family to the wider community beyond'.

Or, in other words, survival.

The Law of Preposterous Precision

The more precise the figures quoted, the less credible they are

'A MILLION VICTIMS of child abuse' ... '75% of the working population have been victims of bullying at work' ... 'not more than three units of alcohol a day' .. 'fifty-six victims of ritual abuse in the Orkneys' ... '60% decline in the UK's thrush population' ... 'so many million at risk from CJD'.

Every day the media solemnly report, with apparently straight faces, figures that are manifestly unbelievable. Every week, organizations equipped with axes that they find too blunt for the purpose of gouging more generous donations from their sympathizers (workers in 'the caring professions' in receipt of insufficient funds to finance their exponentially advancing expectations) conduct tendentious 'surveys' crammed with questions so sloppily worded as to guarantee meaningless results, and release these bogus figures in the 'shock horror' tones of crisis and alarm that they consider necessary to nudge an apathetic public into action.

So, as you munch the frugal two egg-sized potatoes a day recommended by Nanny Bottomley when she was Minister of Health you might care to reflect on the fact that it wouldn't make the slightest difference if they were the size of ostrich eggs, and you consumed twice the recommended quantity, washed down with a reckless six units of château-bottled claret.

No examination of the Law would be complete that failed to mention the closely related Law of

Sanctimonious Prohibition: 'Anything of an enjoyable nature is injurious to health'. This springs from the conviction that, far from doing you a bit of good, a little of what you fancy is probably damaging to health and should never be given the benefit of any doubt that there may be. Any more than a little (which should in no circumstances exceed what, to be clinically and morally precise, may be defined as just the teeniest, weeniest, itsiest, grudging bit) will probably prove fatal, and if it doesn't, could damage your liver and also make you blind.

Such strictures apply to alcohol, gambling, eating, sunbathing, most varieties of sport, watching video and television programmes and all forms of sexual activity (with the sole exception of medically supervised mastur-bation in a licensed fertility clinic.)

Even in a godless, secular society, the old Puritan ethic lives on, has indeed been embraced with unwhole-some and deeply suspect fervour by the medical estab-lishment which, when genuine items of news are in short supply, can be relied on to surface with dire warnings and predictions, many based on the flimsiest and most unreliable research ('a report out today reveals'). Since the days of Hippocrates, doctors have revelled in the reverent compliance of their patients with the medical strictures that they promulgate with an air of such authority. Their sanctimonious confidence seems not to have been dented in the least by the contradictory nature of much medical advice. The solar topee (that ridiculous symbol of empire, seized on with such relish by Noel Coward for his song about 'Mad Dogs and Englishmen') was mandatory in all tropical climes to ward off the dangerous rays of the sun until the embar-rassing discovery was made that it increased the risk of heatstroke. Even red wine has been grudgingly recognized as mildly therapeutic (subject always, of course, to that medical mantra 'in the strictest moderation'). So you can probably take comfort from the likelihood that, one day, your own preferred forms of vice may for a short while find medical favour as capable of doing you some good.

Until then, the safest course to follow is to sit on a hard chair, wearing a hair-shirt to watch video recordings of recent party political broadcasts.

The Coefficient of Insignificance

The resources devoted to a project are in inverse proportion to its significance for profit

Nobody who has ever worked for a company of any size will be unfamiliar with this basic law of management. Everyone can cite examples, ranging from some daft pet project of the chairman's to a bee in the managing director's bonnet which engages the almost exclusive attention of various highly paid members of staff for several days.

I recall working for one of Britain's largest companies as a management trainee in the purchasing department. While I was there, the entire department once spent several days in a frustrating, but ultimately successful, effort to track down an unusual article sought by a senior member of the board: desired he explained, as a wedding present for a relative, the object for which we all combed the country was a 'Long John Silver jug with a parrot handle'.

Apart from the whims of senior colleagues, no project is more likely to be the centre of much attention and activity than anything, however trivial, that is thought to bear upon the important issue of status or prestige, individual or corporate. The sky's the limit when what the Chinese call 'face' is involved. A manager's title, the choice of a logo, the design of a new corporate identity: these are the stuff of endless, protracted meetings and discussions, while the expenditure of a few million pounds on a new computer system goes through on the nod.

The Law of Retromingent Departure

Beware of giving executives an exit interview

CATS ARE PROBABLY the best known of the species whose distinctive habit of urinating backwards is known to zoologists as 'retromingent'. This characteristic use by a departing animal of the full offensive potential of its tail (the skunk is another notable example) is now widely available to vengeful managers on resigning from a company that follows the fashionable human resources practice of conducting exit interviews.

This inauspiciously titled meeting gives departing managers an opportunity to explain in full and even lurid detail the factors that impelled them to resign. And while some may well be content with an exchange of human resources babble about 'lack of career paths' and excessively 'task-oriented' seniors, others will take advantage of the chance to settle a number of scores. It is an interview which, if not conducted skilfully, can lead to accusations of anything from incompetence and lack of vision to bullying and even sexual harassment. An experienced human resources manager, mindful of the retromingent potential of the meeting, will lay in an ample stock of towels and disinfectant, while keeping his interviewee at a sanitary distance.

The Law of Titular Inflation

*The less significant the function the more pretentious
its title*

'TASK FORCE': WHAT kind of mental picture do the
two words conjure up? Battleships and aircraft
carriers speeding into action, escorted by dashing flotil-
las of frigates and destroyers? Squadrons of tanks racing
through a desert sand storm in hot pursuit of a retreat-
ing enemy? And what about 'hit team': soldiers with
blackened faces abseiling down a cliff? Mobsters with
automatic weapons executing a contract on a rival?

More and more often in corporate circles, such terms
are used to camouflage what are essentially committees.
In the stagnant creeks of bureaucratic life these stirring
martial titles have been hijacked by accountants and
people from human resources to lend to their humdrum
and sedentary proceedings a grittily combative flavour.
What would once have been circulated as the minutes of
a staff committee meeting become dynamically remus-
tered as a 'brief' or 'progress report' from the 'staff
morale task force'. Members of the office maintenance
committee (Eddie the painter and Fred the electrician)
find themselves suddenly redesignated as the 'accommo-
dation task force' or the 'relocation hit team'.

Managers who have not yet succeeded in securing a
more impressive title for their own jobs instead inflate
the job descriptions of subordinates, calling secretaries
'personal assistants', for example, or, even better, 'executive personal assistants'. (The prefix 'executive' to an
otherwise commonplace title is offered as compensation
for a disappointing rise in salary).

The Law of Executive Propulsion

The most powerful corporate propellant is the ego

THE MOTIVE POWER of managers is *ego*. Most of them are driven not by calculation or by reason, but by that powerful propellant self-esteem. As a result, an organization only prospers when self and corporate interest coincide. When they come into conflict, considerations of prestige, of 'face', are always bound to prevail.

This elementary fact of life first came to my attention when the firm of publishers I worked for at the time set out to acquire, at no small cost, a relatively small provincial firm. Although engaged in an allied business, it was making very little money; its market was totally different, as were its selling methods and management structure. The reasons for wishing to acquire it were in consequence not obvious.

Though shrouded in portentous management-speak (in which I recall that 'synergy' was a word that figured prominently) it soon became apparent that the real reason for the company wishing to buy it was the wistful desire of the chief executive to savour the ego-boosting experience of taking over another company – the corporate equivalent of a successful seduction. To achieve this ambition (in his view, the high spot of a dull but blameless career) he would cheerfully have taken over a chain of loss-making whelk stalls in Qatar.

Predictably enough, the acquisition was not a great success. Nevertheless the negotiations ate up countless costly man hours, involving as they did an army of bankers, consultants, lawyers and accountants, and the eventual purchase price agreed was huge. The return on this ill-starred investment was, however, peanuts.

What this case history taught me was the invaluable lesson summed up in the law that heads this chapter: greater than influence, profit, growth or any other valid corporate objective are the egos of its senior executives. The closer to their hearts some zany project lies, the greater the resources of money, time and energy that are devoted to it.

Look around you at your office: the chances are that you will see countless other examples of the Law in action.

The Law of Obstructive Creativity

The most popular form of creative work is making difficulties

IN A CORPORATE environment one of the most difficult things to achieve is acceptance of a new idea. And contrary to belief, it is young people who most ferociously resist innovation. This is because in the absence of experience, precedent is their sole criterion for judging the worth of an idea. Feeling safest with what they know already, they cling to the familiar like shipwrecked sailors to a floating spar. Their idea of radical innovation is to find some minuscule variation from accepted practice. This provides an illusion of living dangerously, while at the same time preserving the warm, safe feeling of familiarity.

Such resistance to change and hostility to innovation, is, of course, in the long run death to any organization. But by the time this realization dawns it is usually too late.

The Law of Conceptual Parentage

*An idea whose value has been proved will never be
an orphan*

I FIRST OBSERVED this law in action many years ago
when the American company for which I worked
threw down a challenge to its subsidiaries worldwide.

'Here', they explained, 'is the mailing package that we
currently use on our most profitable product line. Here
too are the results of recent tests that we have mailed.
We now offer a prize (I seem to recall that the sum was
about $500 – this was, after all, many years ago, and the
parent company was never conspicuous for generosity)
for the best idea received from our subsidiaries for
improving results. From the ideas submitted we will
pick those that look most promising, and test them
against our current mailing package and each other'.

Fired by this challenge a colleague and I put our
heads together and, within about two hours, had devised
a package that the UK company submitted. In essence
all that we had done was to combine the elements of two
successful tests that the Americans had themselves run
recently, an idea so obvious that we were astounded
when it eventually proved to be the winner.

However, since we two alone had devised it, we were
both a little surprised at the number of colleagues who
came forward to claim a share of the credit, and, of
course, the $500. The claimants included not only the
head of our department (who had contributed nothing),
but also a typographer (whose contribution had been
confined to selecting the font and size of type), the

designer (who had simply provided a layout for 300 words of copy), and the company messenger (who had posted the result). Each believed with apparently passionate sincerity that his individual contribution to the operation had been crucial to success. So too, but with rather more justification, did my colleague and I.

In order to propitiate the fast-extending queue of claimants, and also to prevent unseemly wrangling about who deserved the credit, the UK company was obliged to match the US parent's original prize-fund, which was eventually shared between about six people.

Since then I have on countless occasions observed the large number of people prepared to claim parentage of others' good ideas, including, quite often, those bent on sharing with me credit for ideas that I had fondly thought of as my own.

The Law of Predictable Redundancies

*The probable scale of redundancies can be accurately
predicted from the number, size and duration of
meetings held by the organization*

PEOPLE *LOVE* MEETINGS. Although they affect irritation and impatience with the number of meetings
they 'have to' attend, the fact is that most enjoy them.
For those who have little or nothing to do, a diary
whose pages are crammed with meetings gives some
kind of orderly structural framework to life, provides a
comforting illusion of being busy, useful, even indispensable. And because they like attending meetings,
they are loath to bring them to a close.

How often have you been present when a meeting
has clearly served whatever purpose it might have had,
and yet the participants show an obvious reluctance to
disperse? They will happily continue to sit around the
table, smiling expectantly at each other, while they wait
patiently for one of their number to say something,
anything, that will serve as an excuse to prolong the
discussion, which will continue in more and more desul-
tory fashion until at last it becomes embarrassingly
evident to all that there is no conceivable excuse not to
bring it to an end.

A less widely recognized feature of meetings is the
fact that their number and duration provide ample
warning, several months in advance, of the probable
scale of redundancies. This is because the less people
have to do that is of any real functional value, the more
time they can afford to spend in meetings. The simple

fact is that, if they had anything more important or useful to do, they would either not be there at all, or would not stay there for as long. The more meetings an organization has, the longer their duration, and the more people who attend them, the more probable it is that, as soon as times get hard, large-scale redundancies will be announced.

One way of reducing attendance at meetings is to hold them in an executive's office, or even at his desk. This helps to keep the meeting small. It bodes ill for the health of an organization when the number and size of the areas set aside for meetings (boardrooms, conference rooms etc.) add up to more than a tiny proportion of the total office space.

The P45 Law

It is only those with no real job to do who are never made redundant

IN OTHER WORDS, the paper-shufflers are the last to go. As a company down-sizes, salesmen, technicians, scientists, creatives, all disappear in droves. But the tides of redundancy seldom encroach on the human resources department. At the drop of a hat these versatile members of staff can switch from writing letters of engagement to producing letters of dismissal, from interviewing job applicants to counselling those who have just been fired.

When an organization decides that it needs to slash costs, you might imagine that a good way to start would be, not to make people redundant, but to cut back on costly marginal activities. Unfortunately, most of these turn out to be of a kind for which the human resources department is responsible (see the **Law of Peripheral Primacy**).

Although all these contribute directly and substantially to costs, and only indirectly, if at all, to profit, they provide the ever-growing ranks of the human resources department with a *raison d'être*. To eliminate any of them would involve job losses where they hurt. The issue of P45s is the one corporate activity that continues up to and even after the moment of brain death.

The Law of Synchronized Freedom

Working hours are automatically adjusted to ensure that minimum staff presence coincides with maximum customer demand

WALK INTO ANY bank during the lunch hour and try to cash a cheque. You will very soon discover that 'recent improvements in the service that we give our customers' have included replacing most of the people with machines. Cash (if the machine is not 'temporarily out of order') is dispensed mechanically from a hole in the wall, while financial advice (much of it partisan and ill-informed) is dispensed by bumptious and ignorant young people seated informally at desks where customers present themselves to grovel for their money. Remaining survivors of 'rationalization' may be observed through the bullet-proof glass, engaged in animated conversation, mouths opening and closing soundlessly like tropical fish in a tank.

It is likely to be some time before one of them swims in your direction; the Law insists that staff take their lunch at the same time as the customers, thus ensuring that both enjoy simultaneous freedom to do anything but cash a cheque.

The Law of Peripheral Primacy

Attention focuses most readily on inessentials

FEW THINGS IN corporate life have the same seductive, magnetically attractive quality as those of supreme unimportance. When profits are plummeting, key staff departing in droves, costs spiralling out of control and output in free-fall, there are few more comforting ways for senior managers to spend time than in debating the merits of designs for a new corporate livery or letter-head, or discussing the precise angle of the arrow or lightning bolt in the company logo.

This enthusiasm for peripheral activities is one of the principal reasons for the growth in size of the human resources department. The vast range of inessential functions and activities which it spawns or sponsors keeps staff occupied contentedly in a variety of harmless ways which, if they do little to address the key issues facing the organization, at least do no actual damage (see **Work Replacement Therapy**).

A large number of these essentially peripheral activities fall within the area of 'training'. One organization's 'menu' of training courses included among other options: 'Developing the Best through Coaching', 'Role of the Manager', 'Managing Time', 'Developing Meeting Skills', 'Report Writing Skills' and 'Presentation Skills'.

Note that not one of these well-meant but time-consuming courses has any specific focus on the actual jobs of the participants. Whether these are in accountancy, sales, information technology or buildings and maintenance, the individuals will learn nothing that equips them to do their jobs in a more professional, effective way. In order to boost attendance figures to a level that justifies the size and cost of the human resources department, nearly all training courses are centred on generalized, soft-focus platitudes of no greater relevance or value to, say, a market researcher than to a secretary. The crucial development and improvement of professional, technical knowledge and performance is neglected in favour of costly peripheral activities.

The same human resources department mentioned earlier, given the task of recruiting an advertising copy-writer, came up with a 1,000-word advertisement that featured a long list of the qualities required of applicants. These included such woolly desiderata as 'excellent interpersonal skills', 'a positive approach' and 'a commitment to excellence'; two indispensable qualifications, writing talent and a flair for selling, didn't even rate a mention.

Issues of managerial status and prestige take automatic precedence over all other concerns: the precise wording of a manager's job description or title, the size and position of offices, the quality and area of the carpets they're permitted, the nature (solid or dotted) of the lines linking boxes on the organization chart: such public manifestations of position in the pecking order are what preoccupy most managers, sometimes more even than salary and profit share, which tend to be more or less 'private'.

The Law of Mutual Munificence

The task of determining the board's emoluments is one that itself commands a generous reward

COMFORTABLY ENSCONCED ON the boards of most substantial companies are one or two dignitaries known as 'non-executive directors'. Although not directly involved with the day-to-day conduct of the business, they nevertheless bear an awesome burden, for to them falls the crucial responsibility of deciding the remuneration of their colleagues.

Unlike MPs whose strong sense of equity and justice has led them to shoulder uncomplainingly the duty of determining their own remuneration, even when (as is so often the case) the public interest demands that they vote themselves a substantial salary increase, company directors are willing to submit to the judgement of their peers and leave to a committee composed of non-executives the task of deciding how much they ought to be paid.

By a strange coincidence, the remuneration that non-execs receive for assuming this key role is decided by other members of the board on whose emoluments they in turn exert such influence. Thus the Law, while permitting a wholly disinterested objectivity, at the same time ensures a pleasing symmetry that is almost symbiotic.

Management Devices

Management Fictions

FACTS ARE ALWAYS intractable and often inconvenient. It is therefore often easier to pretend that circumstances are other than they actually are.

Hence the development of the Management Fiction. If the irresistible force of your ambition is obstructed by the immovable object of a fact, the solution is to act as if it wasn't there. The concept of the Management Fiction will enable you to continue, unimpeded, on your way.

For example, you wish to introduce a job evaluation scheme. One of its main objectives is to establish the ideal of equal rewards for people who do jobs of equal importance to the company, irrespective of the nature of their work, or the department in which it is done. Thus, any job which carries the prefix 'senior' should have the same salary scale whether the incumbent is an accountant or a salesman.

Now, a little thought will soon show that, while it may be possible to establish this kind of parity for some jobs (such as those of plumbers, carpenters and decorators), it will in many cases prove impossible. For example, the profits of a pharmaceutical company depend largely on the success of its research team. How can jobs of equal value be found in the accounts or sales departments?

To solve the problem, therefore, the firm needs a Management Fiction that boldly circumvents impossibilities by insisting that they do not exist. In this case, the appropriate management fiction would be a ringing declaration that all jobs in all departments have their equivalents across the company.

One more example may serve to illustrate the value of fictions to managements beset by inconvenient or disconcerting facts. Suppose for a moment that you run an advertising agency, of which the biggest department is made up of two kinds of people, writers and designers. Some companies (the least progressive and imaginative) might adopt the lazy manager's option of valuing these people individually, and paying each according to their skills, efforts and results.

However, to the progressive manager this would be most unsatisfactory and considered untidy, divisive and élitist. The solution? Make up a Management Fiction; for example, that all creative animals are not only equal, but equally creative in exactly the same kind of way. The beauty of this fiction is that it justifies you in treating all these people as interchangeable. Suppose, for example, that one designer has shown a special gift for designing car advertisements, while another has specialized in ads for perfumes. With your Management Fiction in place you can cheerfully switch them from one kind of job to another, putting the car specialist to work on sexy fragrance ads, and his more ethereal colleague on hard-nosed campaigns for rugged 4-wheel-drive vehicles.

Notwithstanding some minor disadvantages, the Management Fiction will continue to flourish. It makes life easier for managers, saving them the necessity to make individual judgements and painful comparative assessments of value.

Work Replacement Therapy

FOR THIS VALUABLE concept we have to thank the HR people (the initials stand, not for hormone replacement but for human resources, the currently fashionable term for the function once known as personnel). HR do however provide a form of replacement therapy in the shape of a range of corporate activities which supply much needed replacements for work. Not every member of the staff is employed, full time, on useful, productive or profitable work. To occupy the many hours that would otherwise be spent in idle gossip, standing outside the office smoking or simply reading the papers, the human resources department offers various forms of Work Replacement Therapy.

Training

Many of these are described as 'training'. But the forms available are seldom targeted or focused. The descriptions of them are generally vague: 'Communication and Interpersonal Skills', 'Working as One of a Team', 'Leading by Example' and the like. An extensive menu of costly and time-consuming training courses enables employees to be 'trained' to do just about anything except their jobs. 'Personal Development Workshops', 'Performance Management', 'Management Development Programmes' 'Meetings and Communication Skills', 'Managing Time', 'Writing Reports' ... the list is potentially endless, limited only by the ingenuity and ambitions of the human resources director.

Elaborate job evaluation schemes are introduced, soon to be supplemented by performance appraisal. At first, the appraisal moves downward from seniors to subordinates. Before long, however, what is known as 'upward appraisal' too is introduced. Eventually the company's employees spend so many working hours appraising each other's performance that little time is left for the functions whose performance is ostensibly the subject of appraisal.

Work replacement therapy owes much to Displacement Management (q.v.) because displacement activities such as performance reviews and job evaluation themselves create a necessity for training. Thus hours can be harmlessly occupied, not just in reviewing performance and evaluating jobs, but also in workshops on 'Managing Performance' and 'Job Evaluation Skills'.

Communication Meetings

You wander the corridors disconsolately in search of somebody capable of answering your question or helping with your problem. But all the offices you enter are deserted, apparently abandoned in haste by their occupants. Traces of recent occupancy are still evident: lights are on, desks are strewn with papers, VDU screens still cast a baleful glow. But all the users are absent; trilling telephones remain unanswered. Is there not, you wonder, someone – anyone – in this entire goddam department with whom you can do business? Or has the place been stricken by a neutron bomb?

From a passing messenger you learn the reason for everybody's absence. The whole department is, it seems, at a 'communication meeting'. And in case the term is unfamiliar I should perhaps explain that a communication meeting is the corporate equivalent of what used in more sexist times to be known as a mothers' meeting – an assembly at which those present allow their minds to drain by the simple expedient of opening their mouths; a rabbit-fest which goes on and on at interminable length because none of those sitting round the table can ever have their fill (and also because the only possible alternative is work).

The ostensible and admirable function of the departmental communication meeting is to provide a forum for the exchange of information and ideas, for managers and staff to engage in amicable and productive dialogue about what and how the company is doing, for complaints to be aired, questions answered and suggestions made. In practice, what usually happens is that the meeting is hijacked by the departmental troublemaker, a strident paranoid smoking room lawyer whose entire working life is dedicated to finding and exposing evidence of management skulduggery.

Brainstorming

The form of corporate activity known, misleadingly, as 'brainstorming' is an increasingly popular form of Work Replacement Therapy. The practice must have originated in a rueful acknowledgement of the fact that, while new ideas are the life-blood of a business, not many people are able to recognize a good idea, and even fewer are capable of having one. From this, by some logical process that is difficult to follow, arose the strange belief that something of which individuals seem incapable can more easily be accomplished by a group (much as a table too heavy to be lifted by one is believed to be capable of levitation by the application of several people's fingertips). Thus meetings are held to 'brainstorm' ideas of every conceivable kind, from books to advertising concepts, from ways to raise money for charity to solutions to marketing problems.

Unfortunately, few 'brainstorming' sessions generate enough creative turbulence to fill a teacup.

Management Euphemisms

A MANAGER FOR whom I worked early on in my career hit on an ingenious way to hoodwink members of his staff into accepting disagreeable assignments willingly. Giving you one of his most sincere and candid stares he would lean towards you and murmur in confidential tones 'I want to ask your advice'.

Flattered as I always was by this request, it took me a long time to cotton on to the fact that the advisory role invariably seemed to involve, indeed, to consist primarily of some unusually thankless chore.

However, I soon caught on to the fact that people are usually far more co-operative if the work that you give them can be camouflaged as something else – help, an opinion, or, of course, advice. It is also more acceptable if you can plausibly pretend that nobody else is so well qualified to do it. In this connection 'your special expertise' and 'the unrivalled experience that you have' are both useful phrases.

An outstanding example of Management Euphemisms came my way not long ago in the shape of a letter from the chairman of the Institute of Direct Marketing. This brought me an invitation (which the letter suggested quite correctly I might find 'rather flattering') to become what was impressively described as a 'Founder Member'. It went on to massage my ego in even warmer terms: 'The fact is that you have played an outstanding part in the development of direct marketing. Indeed, I do not think I would be contradicted if I said you are one of the *shapers* of the business, having helped put UK direct marketing in the forefront of European practice'.

Only some paragraphs later did I come to the pill so skilfully embedded in the sugar: 'Of course, the Institute has few reserves and so, alas, Founder Membership cannot be free. But it is for a lifetime. Ordinary Members will pay an annual fee of £70. Founders will pay a once-only fee of £500.'

The experienced Euphemism Manager knows that the human capacity to lap up flattery is virtually limit-less.

Management Rhetoric

THE RHETORIC OF management becomes easier to understand once you recognize its function. Often this is self-congratulation, as in so many situations vacant ads, the unctuously ponderous tone of which is dictated by the writer's need to impress not only potential applicants, but also the world at large (and, not least, himself) with the importance and achievements of the company and the superior status of those fortunate enough to work for it.

Excellence and brilliance are the least of our demands on those who have the personal qualities of dedication, vision, loyalty, entrepreneurial and interpersonal skills – along with a total commitment to success in the highly competitive field of Waste Development. Poised as we are at the leading edge of Waste Technology, we are constantly extending the frontiers of Waste, financial, temporal and human, into territory where few other firms have been bold enough to venture. Under the inspirational leadership of a team internationally renowned for its hard-driving ascent of the pinnacles of Waste, we seek highly motivated individuals with a track record of wasteful achievement. We are an Equal Opportunities, environmentally and socially sensitive employer whose employment policies recognize no distinction of race, religion, sex or intellect. Good communication skills, verbal, non-verbal, olfactory and tactile, are a *sine qua non* for membership of our multi-national, multi-disciplinary team.

The second rhetorical function is often *camouflage*, as in the case of staff announcements, the stately cadences of which convey to skilled interpreters some hidden message about sudden and often dramatic shifts in the power and status of senior employees.

In the hands of a skilled rhetorician, a boardroom convulsion resulting in the loss by an ambitious manager of huge swathes of an empire that it has taken years to build can read like a well deserved promotion.

> William has asked to be relieved of his responsibilities for sales and marketing in order to be able to concentrate his outstanding talents and formidable energies on the essential functions of vehicle and building maintenance. Please join me in congratulating William and wishing him every success in this key appointment.

Or again:

> Following an epic struggle with the adverse trading conditions of recent years, Colin has decided that the time has come to leave us in order to be able to devote more time to his beloved Siamese cats, and his lifelong passion for morris-dancing. He takes with him the admiration of us all for the stubborn courage with which he has resisted change, and not least for the determination with which he has implemented our downsizing, out-sourcing and out-placement programmes which together have made it possible for a slimmer, fitter company to move into new compact headquarters in the agreeable environment of Hackney.

Ambitious managers would be well advised to hone the skills with which they handle the orotund phrases of the rhetorician.

Management Perversions

Bondage

ONE SYMPTOM OF the troubled times we live in is management's craving for rules by which to abide, regulations to which to adhere. The waning influence of religion has created in the ranks of management a need for secular forms of restraint. In the absence of self-discipline, this need is met by codes of practice. As if the restrictions imposed by Brussels and Whitehall were not enough, managements which cannot trust themselves to deal honestly and fairly with customers, society and staff submit eagerly to the thongs and buckles of voluntary bondage.

Few companies would now be seen dead in the market without including in their advertisements and stationery an impressive array of logos proclaiming their adherence to any number of trade associations with high-sounding codes of practice. These are displayed for admiration like trophies on a mantelpiece, or campaign medals pinned to a military chest. Dry cleaners have a code, and so do publishers. There are probably codes in the pipeline for hat-steamers, lollipop vendors and peddlers of soft porn. From pizza houses to massage parlours, from fruit machines to picketing, there will soon be few kinds of human enterprise unencumbered by the stipulations of a code of practice.

Managers who abide by these codes are amply rewarded for their diligence. For the objective of the draftsmen was apparently no less than that of saving managers the need to take any decisions in the troubled field of ethics; indeed, many of the codes go even further, sparing adherents all the perplexities and pain involved in thinking for themselves about such controversial matters as truth, honesty, equity and justice. Reading of all the things their members are sternly enjoined not to do, one gets a somewhat surprising view of British commerce as being made up of companies which cannot trust themselves with customers. They call to mind the deviant who begs to be locked up for his own good.

Fetishism

Just as some sexual deviants are turned on by such unlikely objects as parasols and shoes, there are not a few managements which derive strange satisfaction from contemplating the company's stationery and logo. The pleasure is heightened for some by the heated debates that can take place about the various proposals submitted by design consultants. As with other forms of perversion, indulgence can prove to be a costly pleasure, involving as it does reprinting all the corporate stationery from letterheads to bills, and repainting the entire fleet of vehicles or aircraft. In fact the choice of a new logo is probably one of the biggest financial decisions a manager can take (the design consultancy's fee alone probably exceeds the aggregate annual emoluments of the directors). The total irrelevance of the decision to companies' profits and progress is a source of additional pleasure; what could be more enjoyable than spending millions on something so frivolous and unimportant as, say, replacing BT's former 'morse code' logo with a classical allusion that must be entirely lost on the majority of customers persuaded that it is 'good to talk'.

However, fetishism 'beats masturbation' as one

senior manager was heard to remark following a lengthy meeting to consider alternative logos.

Transvestism

Although far from being everybody's cup of tea, the prospect of dressing up in other people's clothes has, for some managers, a powerful appeal. Almost every day the business section of your daily newspaper will feature at least one photograph of a company director simpering with embarrassed pleasure at being caught in the act of dressing up in someone else's clothes.

The chosen attire does not always have to be of a kind associated with the other sex; the sight of male managers in drag is still relatively rare. But in these days of sexual equality there can be no excuse for flinching from the sight of the male chief executive of a firm that manufactures lingerie dressing up in a bra and pantihose to launch a new line of undergarments.

At the moment, the most popular form of cross-dressing features the characteristic clothing of the work-force. Thus, safety helmets are favoured in the construction industry, while the directors of bakeries and supermarket chains opt for white overalls and canvas trilbies. The act of being photographed in someone else's clothes provides some managers with pleasures no less keen than other people find in bed. Often the chosen pose is symbolic of some corporate event: for example, the merger of two companies may well be announced to the world with a photograph of the two chief executives on a tandem bicycle. Indeed, photographers vie with each other to coax compliant managers into ever more bizarre and ridiculous poses. A company that has just won a council's waste disposal contract might choose to dress the managing director as a dustman and have him photographed carrying a dustbin on his shoulders. This gives the subeditor a peg on which to hang facetious captions: 'Roger Spalding shoulders the burden of increased responsibility', or 'Amalgamated Portfolios' Fileas Fogg carries the can for expansion'.

Dressing up and gurning at the camera is a harmless management perversion that affords much innocent pleasure to many – a welcome diversion from the daily grind of making bad decisions.

Voyeurism

Managers in the grip of this pitiable perversion invariably suffer from an allied condition known as 'scoptophilia' (which dictionaries define as 'a morbid desire to witness the taboo'). Insulated by substantial salaries from what passes for real life, managers make little first-hand contact with consumers. What little they know of their customers' preferences, tastes and habits is therefore gleaned largely from studying sales statistics and market research reports.

Highly prized, therefore, are occasional rare opportunities to see and hear consumers engaged in what market researchers know as 'focus group research' . At these meetings, half a dozen or so consumers considered to be typical of the client's target market are assembled round a table and invited to discuss the company's services or products. Since the presence of people who work for the company is thought to be a possible distraction, its representatives are allowed to observe the proceedings only through a two-way mirror of the kind said to be popular in brothels. The ribald resemblance is heightened by the kind of premises in which these exercises are generally held – typically, a house in some convenient suburb let for the purpose by its owner, a compliant housewife who thereby earns a useful extra income in return for the use of her house and a tray of some refreshing beverage for participants.

Invisible behind their sound-conductive mirror, and sworn to silence, the watching managers achieve some strange form of commercial arousal from watching and listening to customers who often pull no punches in abusing the firm and its products (a form of commercial masochism that many find exciting).

The perverted use to which these homes are put is suspected only by experienced observers who manage to draw conclusions from the number of people dressed in shabby raincoats who disappear inside for hours, emerging later with a look of exhausted satisfaction.

Management Rituals

Most forms of social activity evolve distinctive forms of ritual. These elaborate ceremonies command huge affection and respect, demanding as they do of all participants the scrupulous observance of universally accepted procedures. Much of the pleasure to be derived from such ceremonies stems from the unchanging nature of the familiar proceedings.

One of the favourite rituals of management is known to all who attend it as 'the brief' – equal in popularity only to its counterpart, 'the debrief'.

The origins of both brief and debrief can be traced to the primitive commercial urge to see into the consumer's mind. This brought into being a form of sorcery known as 'market research', the practitioners of which derive a comfortable living from promising gullible and superstitious marketers that market research will enable them to penetrate the innermost, most secret thoughts of those who constitute 'the market'. To assist in this process, another time honoured ritual has been developed known as 'focus-group research'. This involves assembling round a table half a dozen people thought to be fairly typical of whichever market they are there to represent. After a little ice-breaking small talk about some irrelevant subject, the real topic of the day (let us say baked beans) is broached by the researcher. The group are invited to open their minds and mouths on the subject of baked beans: where they buy them, what they like about them, where and when they eat them, to whom they serve them. Shape, colour, texture are exhaustively discussed; no aspect of the subject is ignored. If at any time the animated conversation flags, the presiding researcher will expertly revive it by introducing some new angle, such as the flavour of the sauce in which the beans are bathed.

Throughout the discussion a tape recorder turns discreetly in the background, recording the contributions of each participant. Not a word that is uttered goes uncaptured, because liberal use will later be made of these quotations when the time comes to reveal them at 'the debrief'. This is the ceremony, commanding huge attendance, at which all members of the client's organization who can crowd into the room assemble to listen in an awed and reverent silence, as the research team reveals to them the authentic 'voice of the consumer'. Many of the client's staff spend their lives in sheltered seclusion that effectively insulates them from any form of contact with those who buy their services or products. Consequently opportunities presented by the debrief to hear (as it were, through a medium) voices from 'the other side' are extravagantly prized, and the quotations accorded a respect that would not be inappropriate for the Word of God.

Management Mantras

As in many other social and religious groupings, mantras and incantations have a significant role to play in corporate life. Clichés as most of them are, their very familiarity is comforting; like all clichés they constitute a form of shorthand that often eliminates the necessity for deeper thought and a more considered utterance.

'Level Playing Field'

This desirable piece of rhetorical real estate figures largely in the speeches of directors who resent all forms of competition, particularly those in which a rival has contrived to gain an arguable advantage.

'World Class'

Companies that succeed in selling their products or services abroad yearn for the status (if not the problems) of being in the World League's Premier Division – up there with the BAs, BPs and BTs of this world, the corporate Joneses with whom the remainder would love to keep up, and in whose company they yearn to be seen.

'Leading Edge'

An interesting example of the use of an antonym to describe a company's position in the progress stakes. Firms such as IBM, Boeing and Marks & Spencer, which are genuinely in the forefront of progress, do not need to describe themselves as being 'at the leading edge'. It is therefore usually only pretentious second-raters, many of them still struggling to come to terms with yesterday's technology, who feel the need to describe themselves in this portentous way.

'Managing Change'

A phrase much in vogue to convey an impression of dynamic adaptability. Its frequent and repetitious use betrays an uneasy awareness that the world is changing fast in ways that are often hard to cope with. It also helps to conceal the fact that the only change some people are capable of managing is the kind they tip out of their pockets onto the dressing table every night.

The Controlled Fiasco

FROM THE PERILOUS world of bomb disposal, management has contrived to borrow, and adapt, the imaginative concept of the controlled (or managed) explosion.

To the bomb-disposal expert, the controlled explosion is a small-scale but often spectacular event, deliberately staged in order to prevent the occurrence later of a bigger bang. In its management mutation, the Controlled Fiasco, what might have been only a minor event is diligently managed to the point where it assumes the proportions of a catastrophe.

What distinguishes the managed form from the uncontrolled variety is, firstly, the fact that it can nearly always be foreseen; secondly, its awe-inspiring scale; and, thirdly, the crucial element that at every stage it remains under the strictest management control.

It is in the financial and legal sectors that the Managed Fiasco is most frequently encountered. A splendid example of the latter is afforded by the case of one Szymon Serafinowicz, who was prosecuted recently (and of course unsuccessfully) for war crimes.

Now, as can easily be foreseen, a prosecution launched more than half a century after the alleged events (which in any case took place in another country) against an 86-year-old who suffers from Alzheimer's disease is certain to be unsuccessful. The distinctive achievement of management was, however, to spend £4 million on bringing a case that the Court flung out without a trial.

The Crown Prosecution Service is not, however, the sole exemplar of the Controlled Fiasco. Their closest rivals, the Serious Fraud Office, have been no less committed to failure on a truly epic scale, as notably in the trial of Kevin Maxwell. The dedication shown by legal managers to the Controlled Fiasco has been closely paralleled by financial management. Here, the plethora of controls, ranging from compliance officers through to such regulatory organizations as IMRO, LAUTRO, FIMBRA and the SIB – now amalgamated beneath the mighty umbrella of the PIA – and, in the last analysis, the Bank of England itself, has ensured that whenever financial catastrophe threatens (as it did for example in the cases of Barings, BCCI and the Mirror Pension Fund) it would always be managed to achieve its full potential.

Inspired by such examples in the public sector, far-sighted managers in industry and commerce are beginning to grasp the many opportunities on offer for exploiting the concept of the Controlled Fiasco.